FREDDY
STORIES

to my family

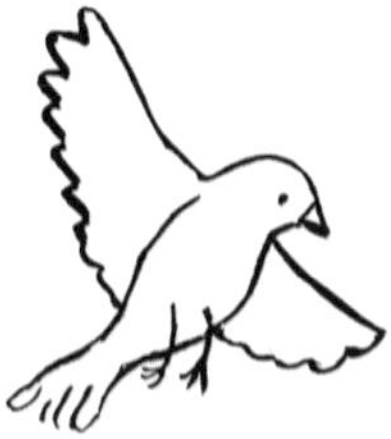

SLAPJACK

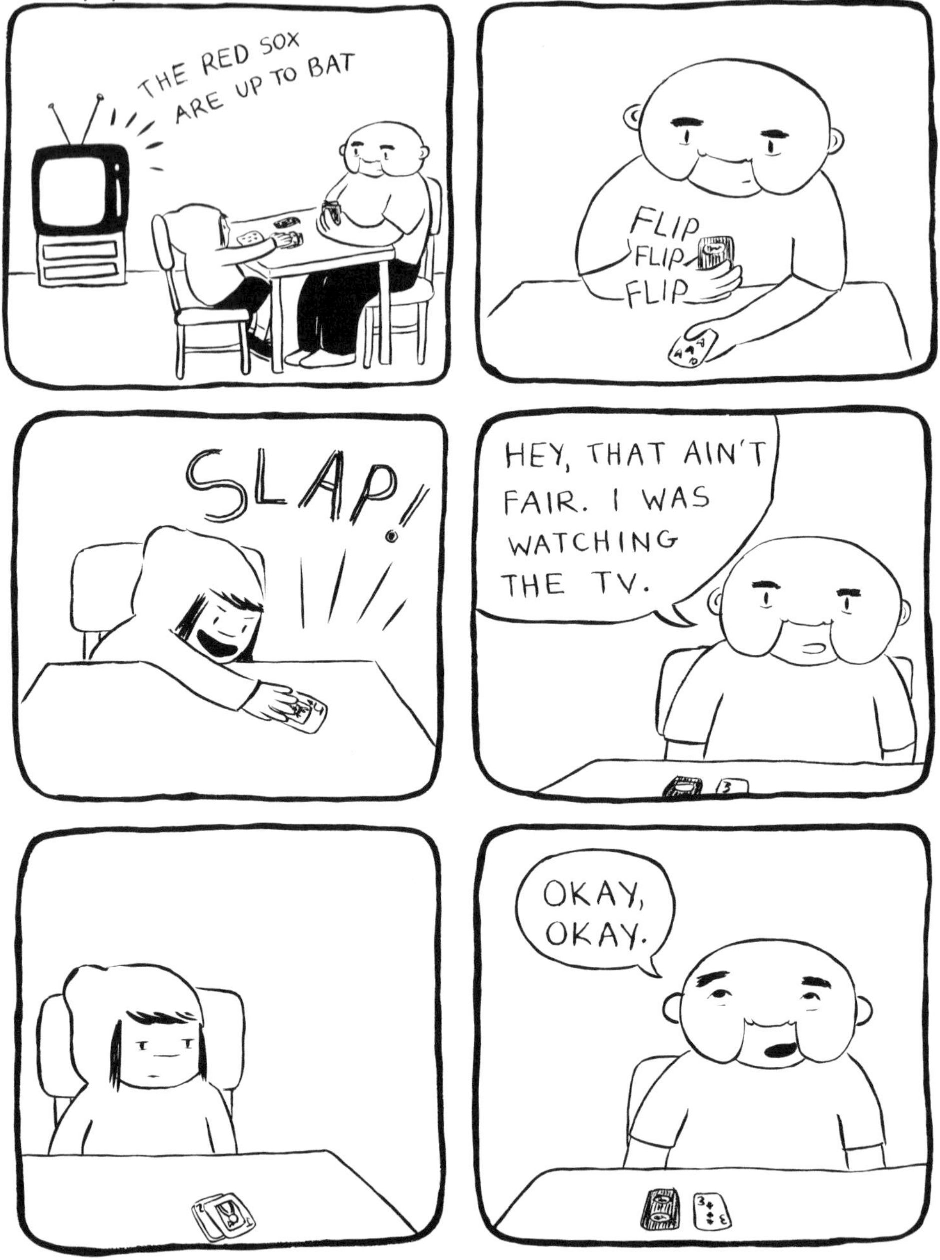
THE RED SOX ARE UP TO BAT
FLIP FLIP FLIP
SLAP!
HEY, THAT AIN'T FAIR. I WAS WATCHING THE TV.
OKAY, OKAY.

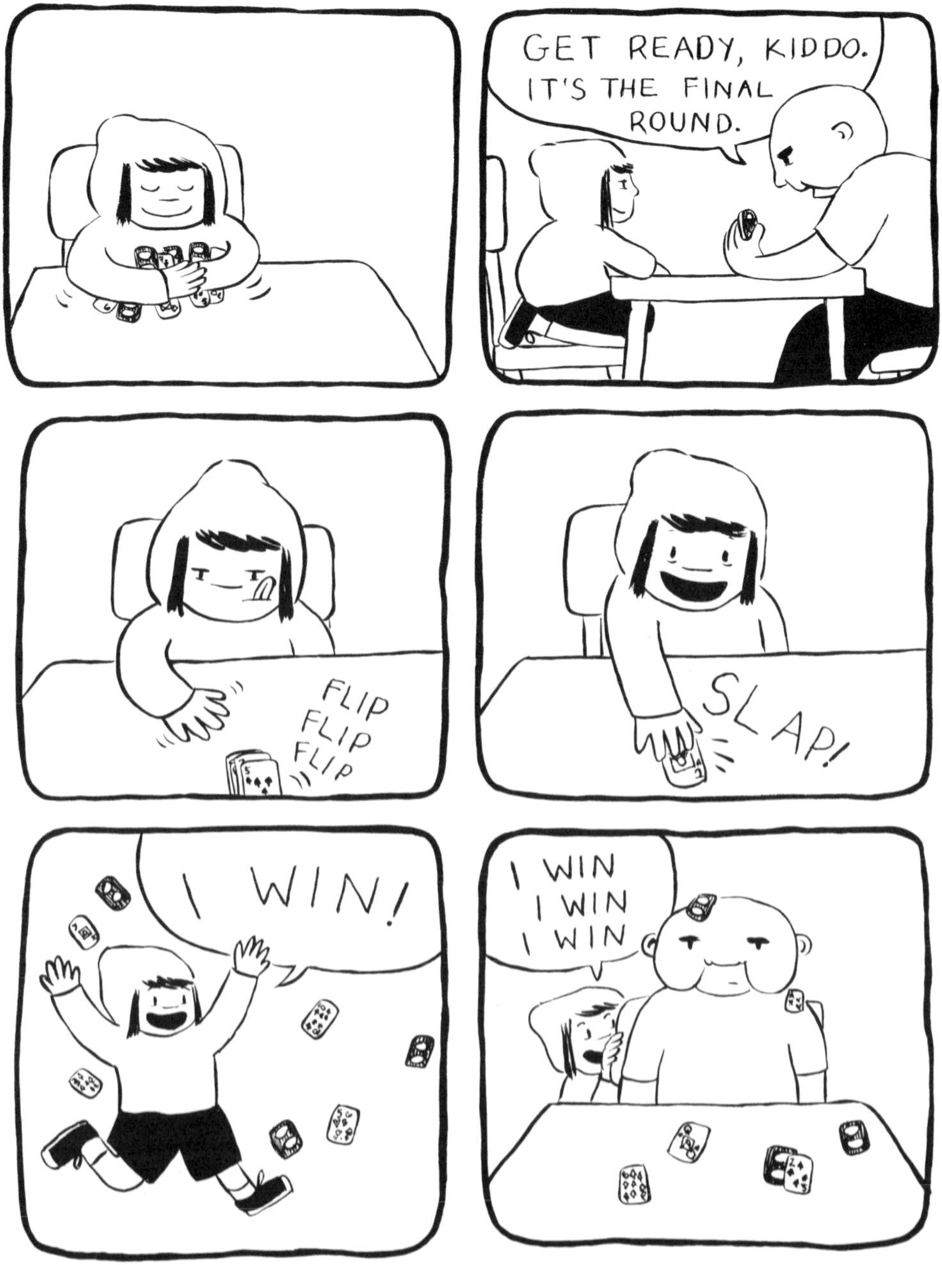
GET READY, KIDDO. IT'S THE FINAL ROUND.
FLIP FLIP FLIP
SLAP!
I WIN!
I WIN I WIN I WIN

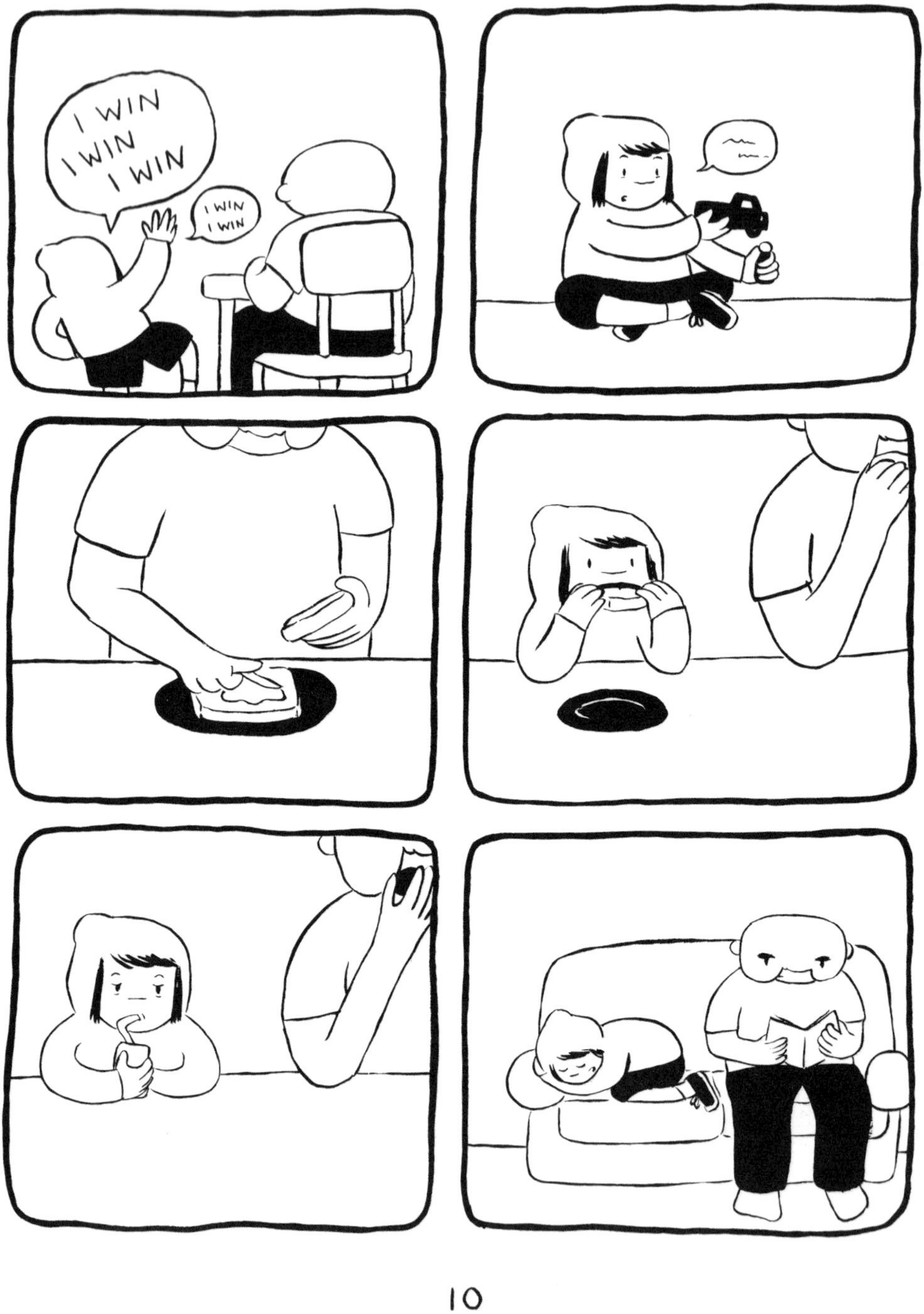
I WIN I WIN I WIN
I WIN I WIN

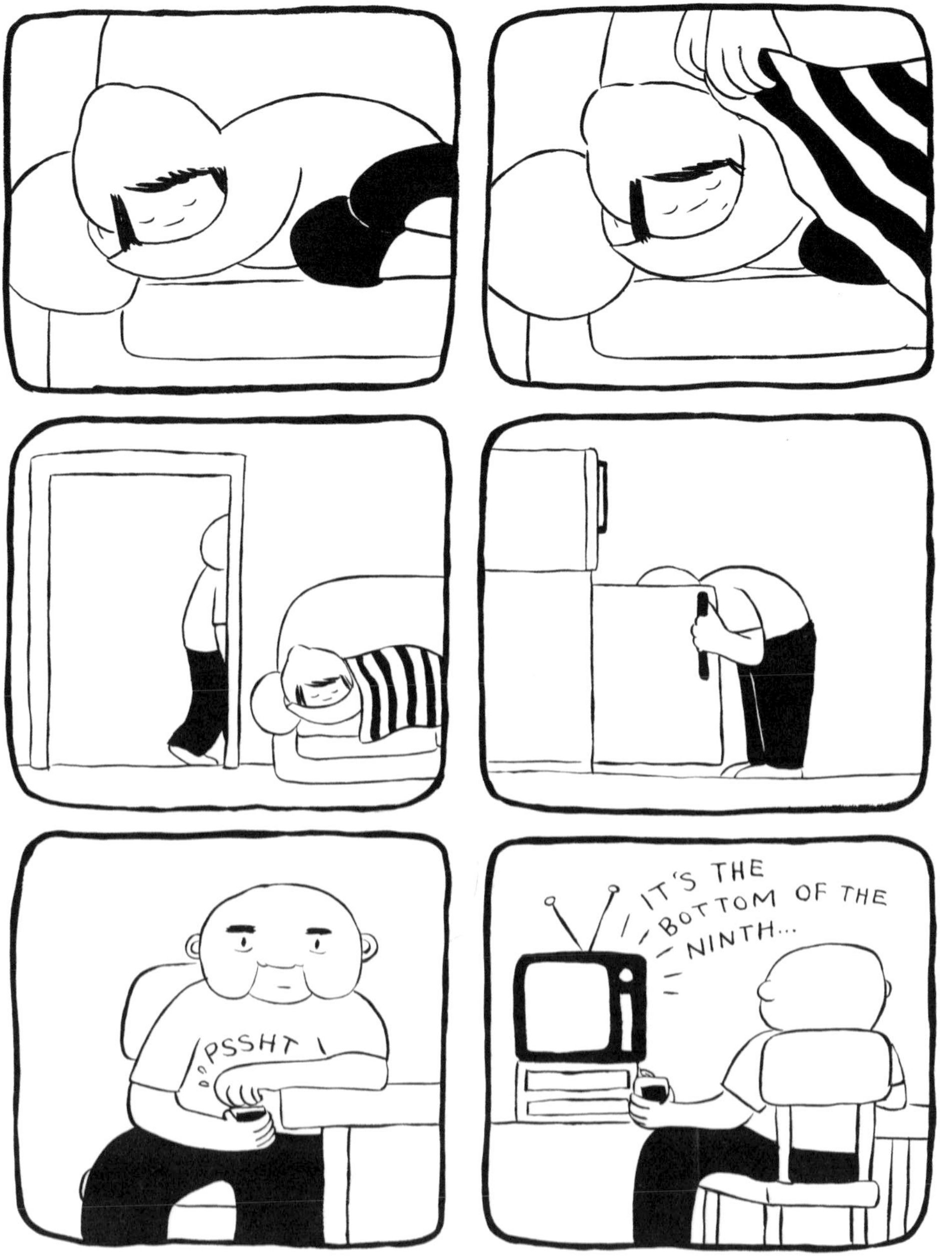
PSSHT
IT'S THE BOTTOM OF THE NINTH...

THE BOYS

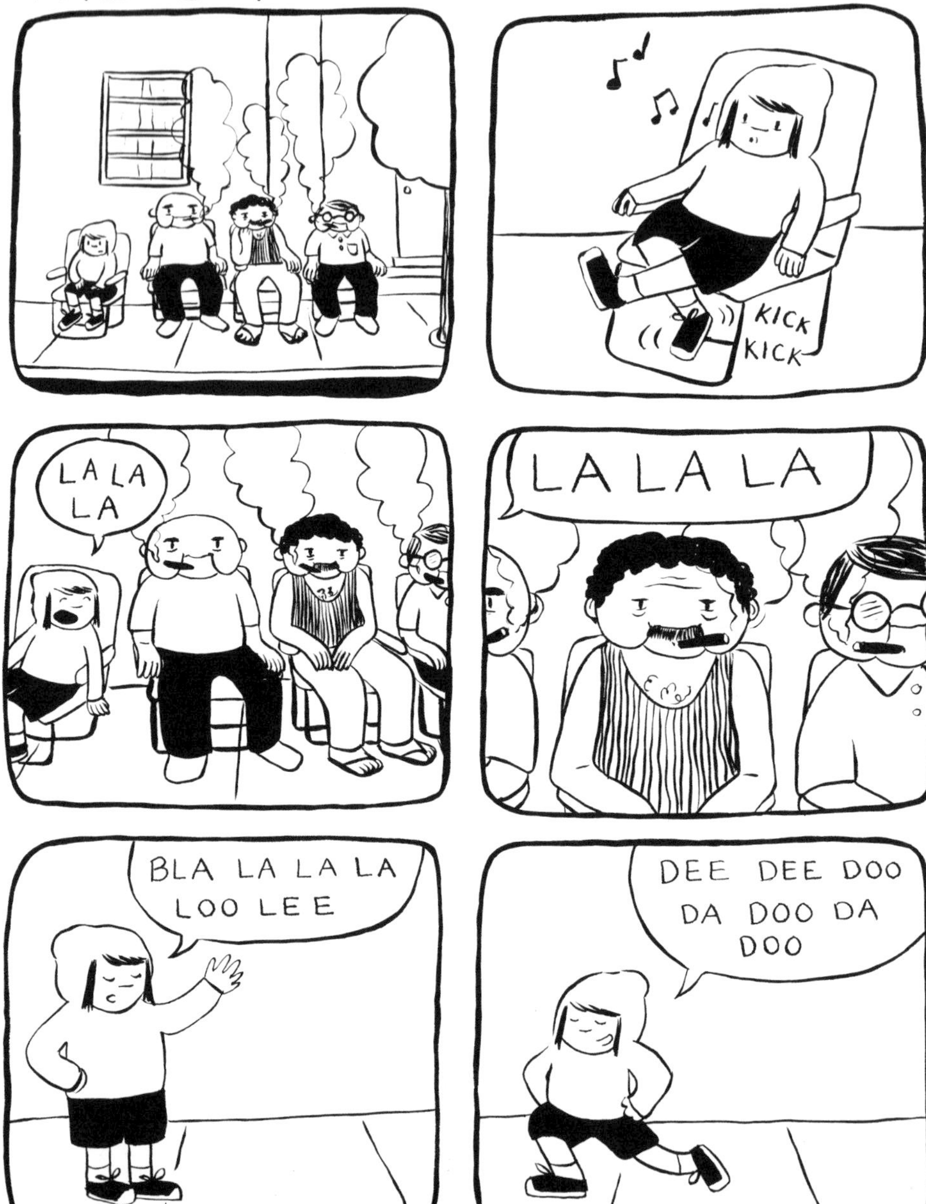
KICK
KICK
LA LA LA
LA LA LA
BLA LA LA LA LOO LEE
DEE DEE DOO DA DOO DA DOO

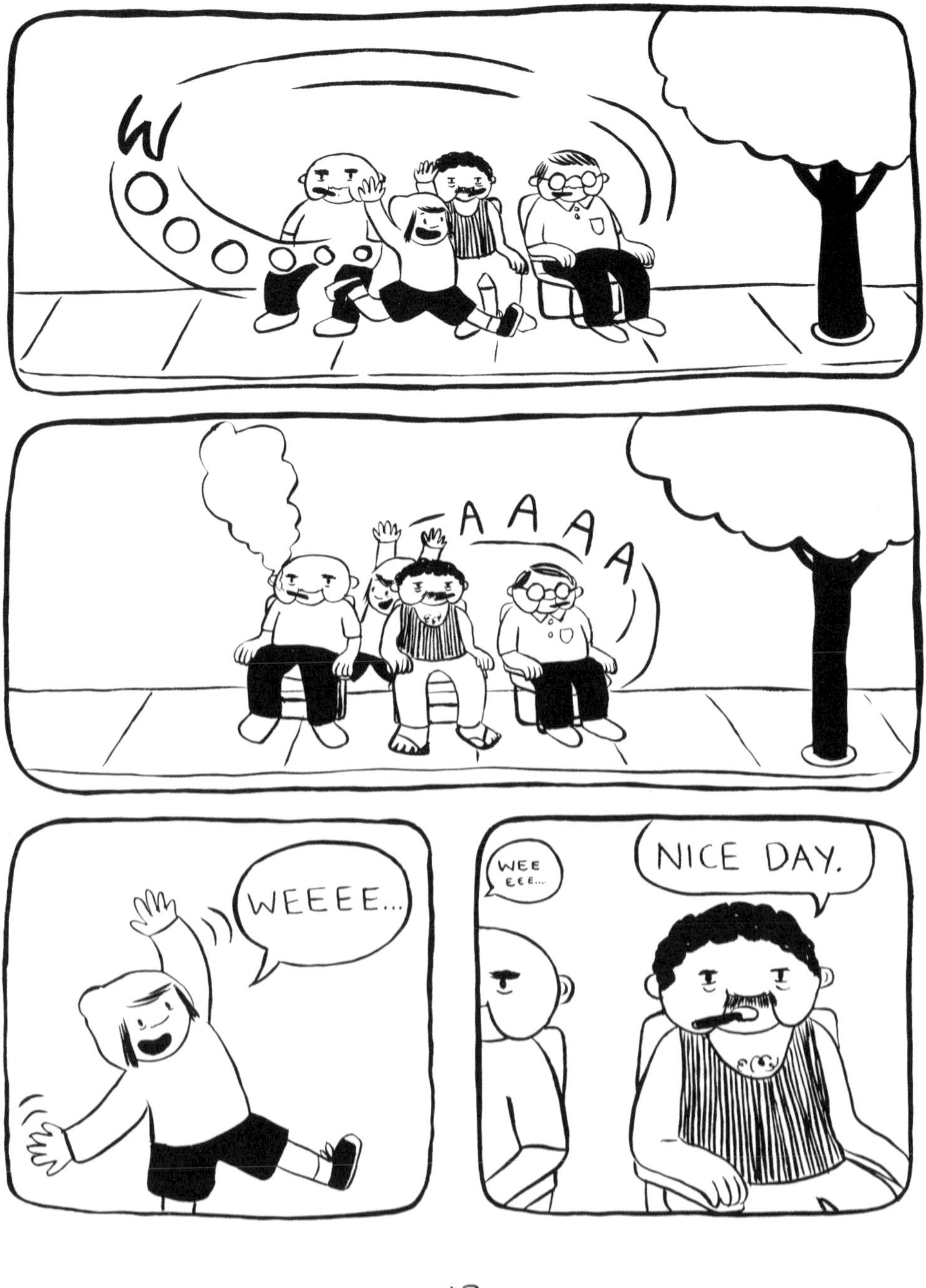
WOOOOOO
AAAA
WEEEE...
WEE EEE...
NICE DAY.

UNCLE SULLY

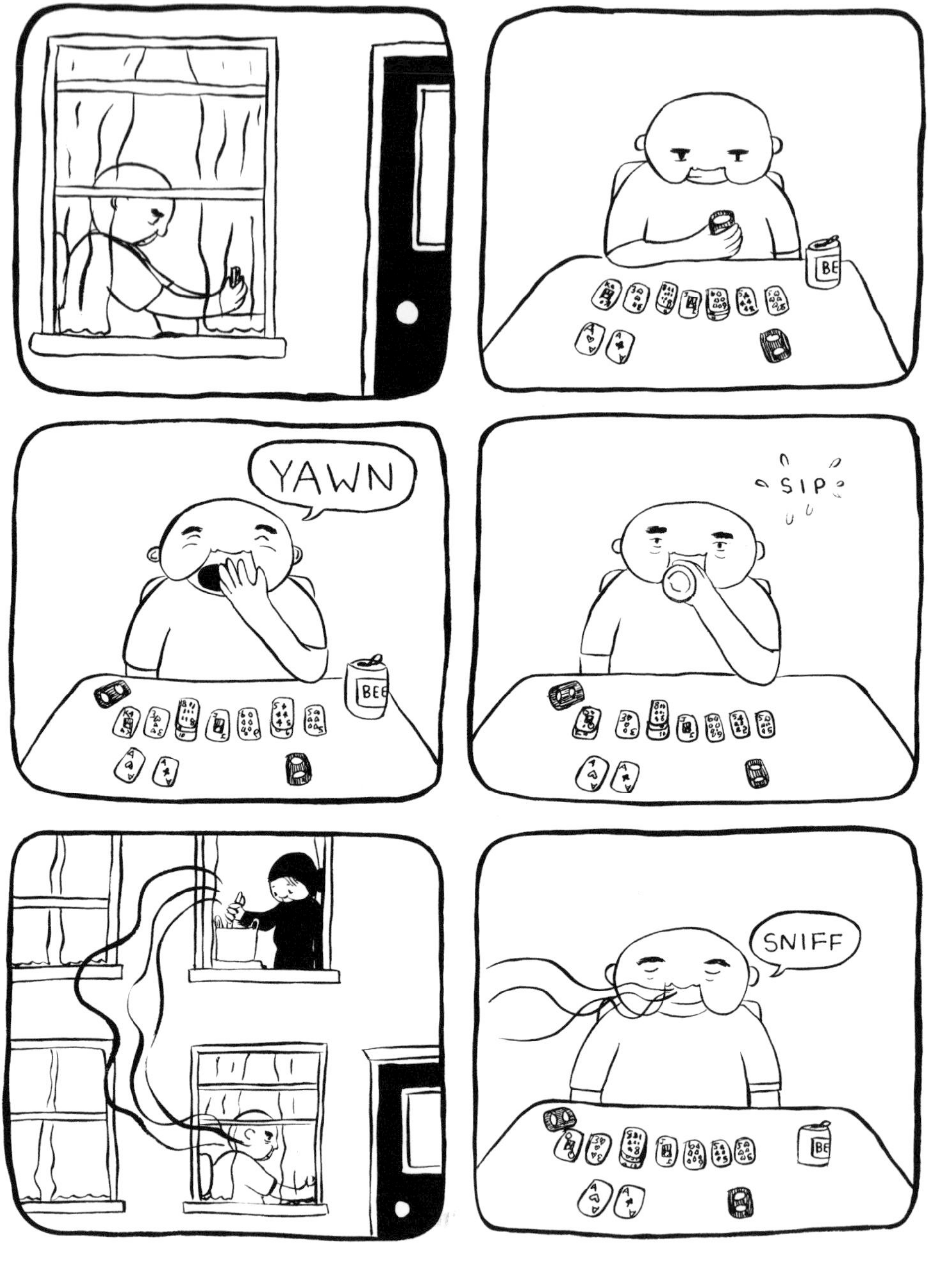
BE
YAWN
BEE
SIP
SNIFF
BE

THE BEACH

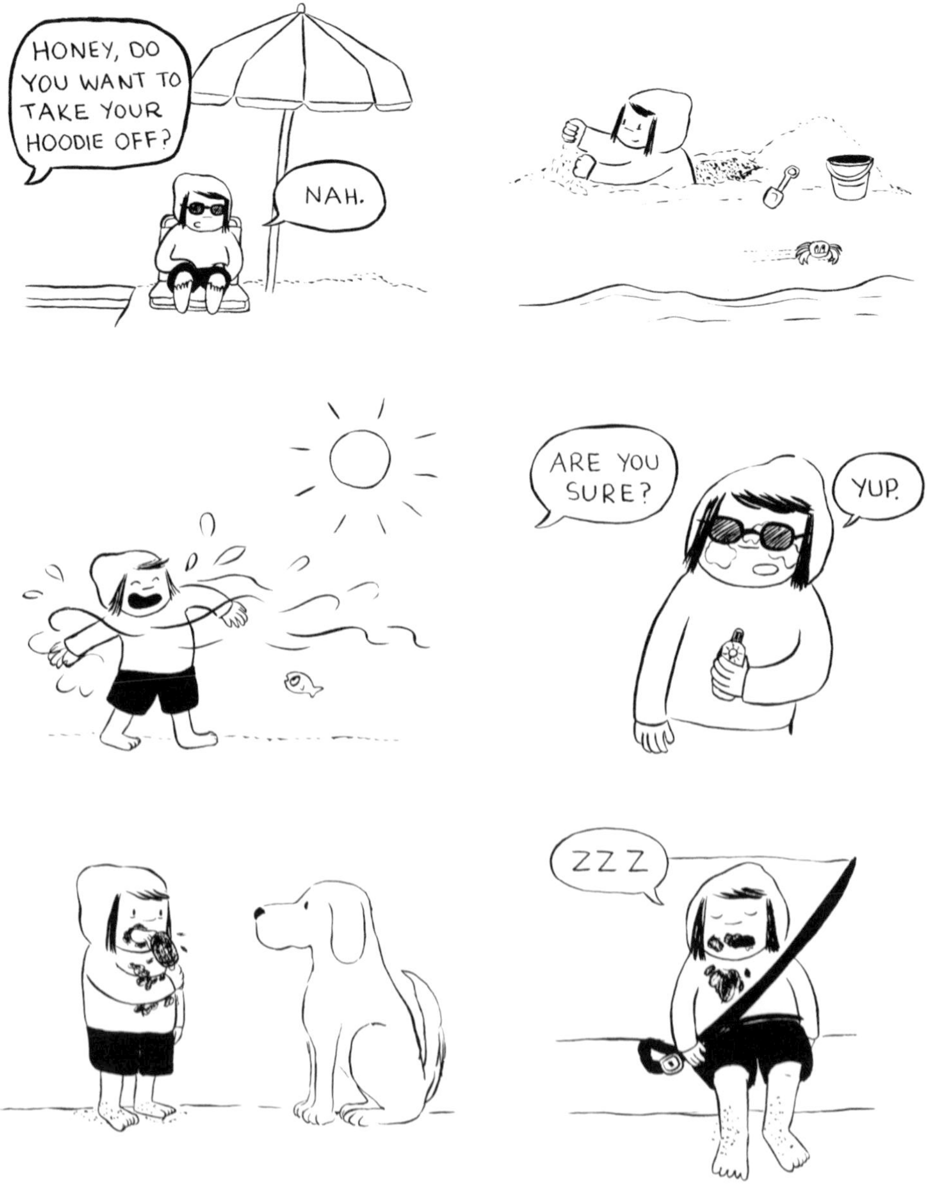

HONEY, DO YOU WANT TO TAKE YOUR HOODIE OFF?
NAH.
ARE YOU SURE?
YUP.
ZZZ

FREDDY AND STEVEN

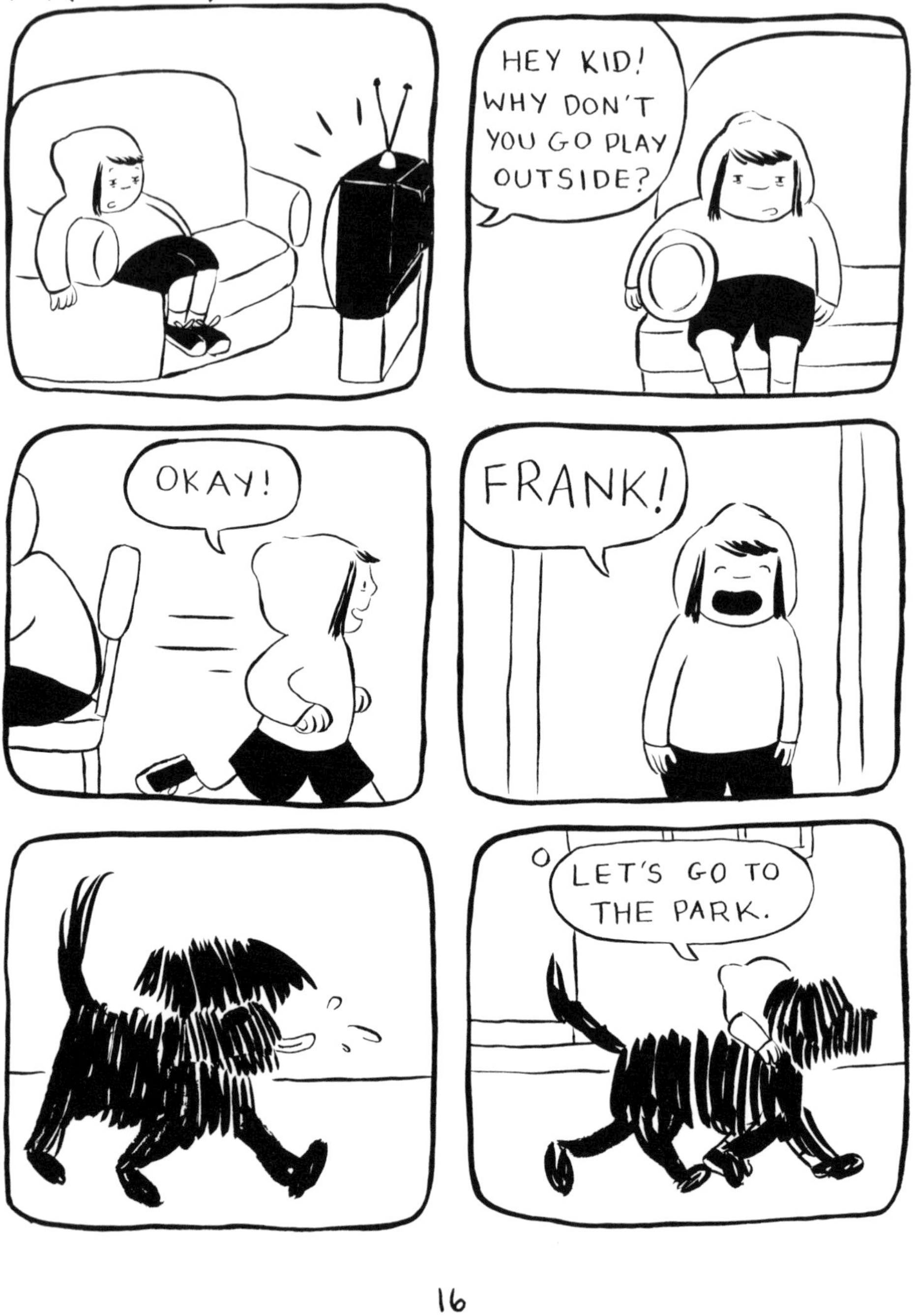

HEY KID! WHY DON'T YOU GO PLAY OUTSIDE?
OKAY!
FRANK!
LET'S GO TO THE PARK.

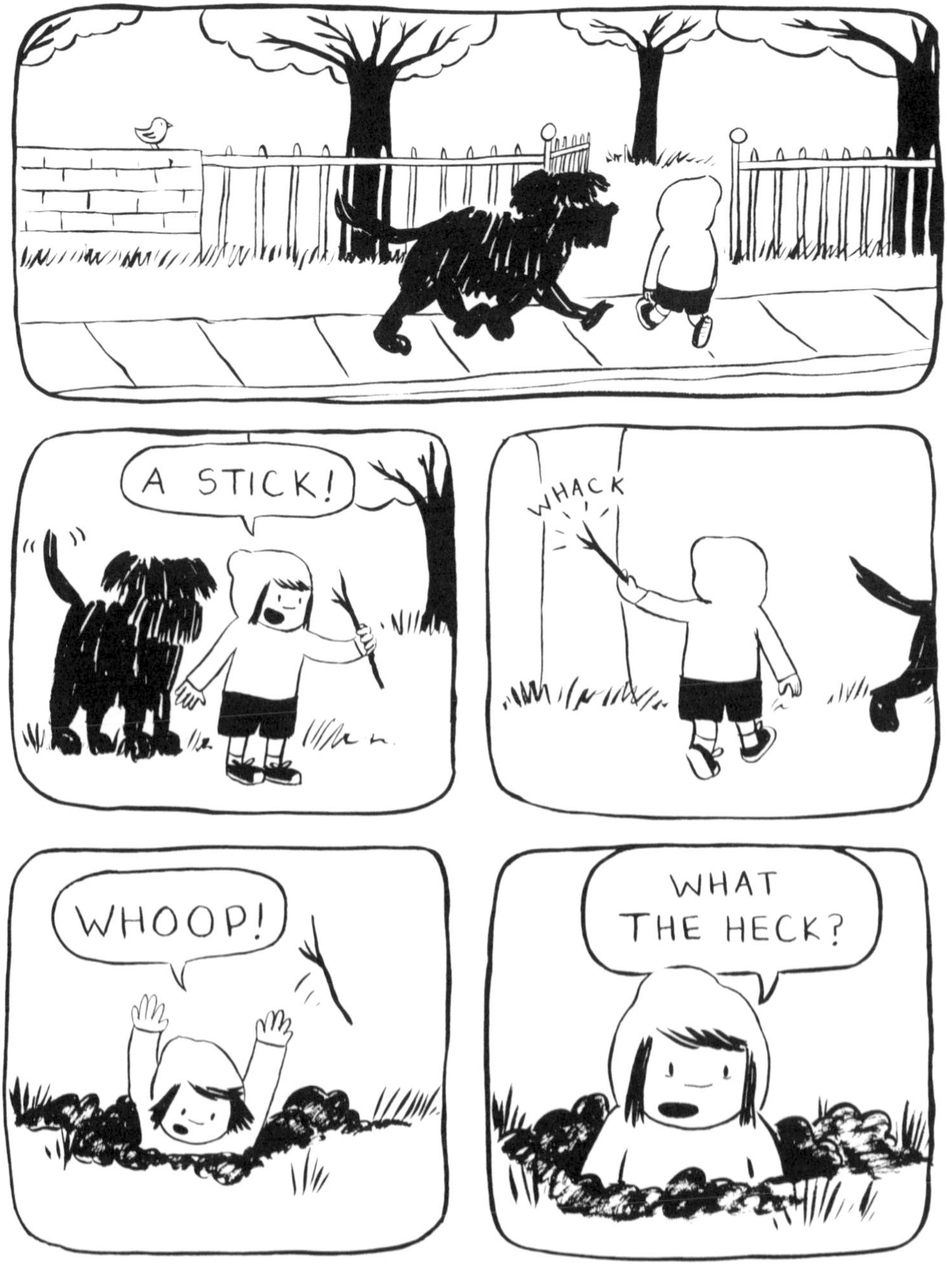
A STICK!
WHACK
WHOOP!
WHAT THE HECK?

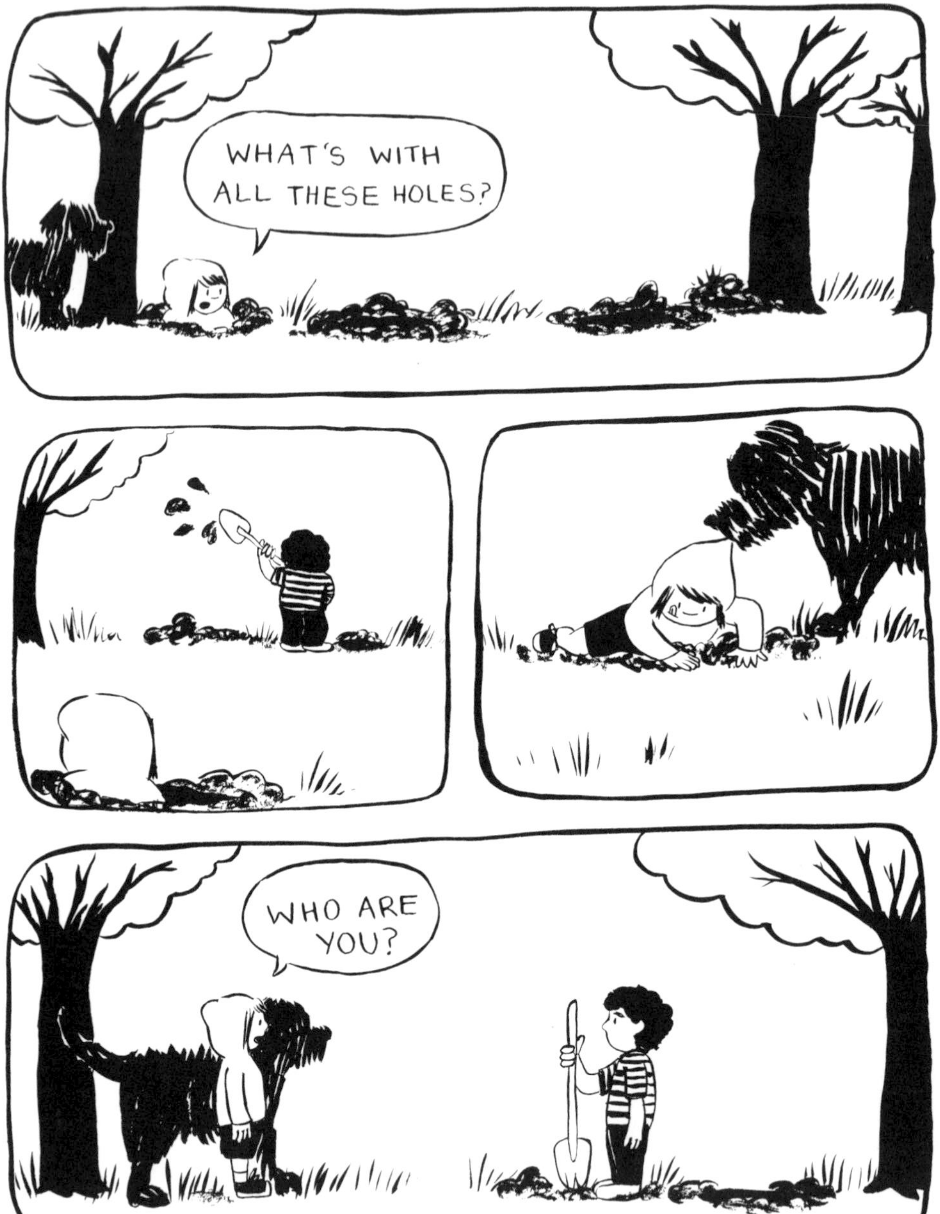
WHAT'S WITH ALL THESE HOLES?
WHO ARE YOU?

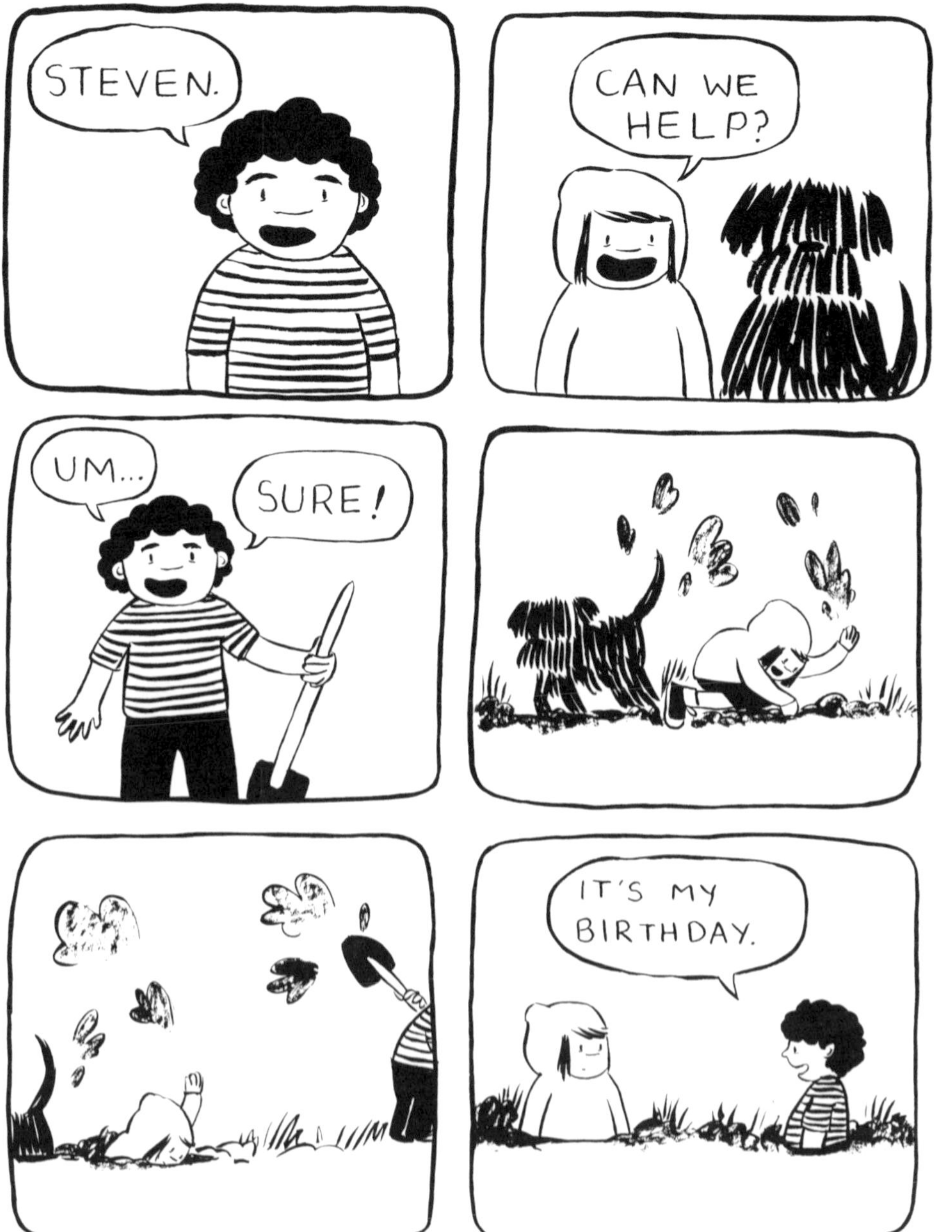
STEVEN.
CAN WE HELP?
UM...
SURE!
IT'S MY BIRTHDAY.

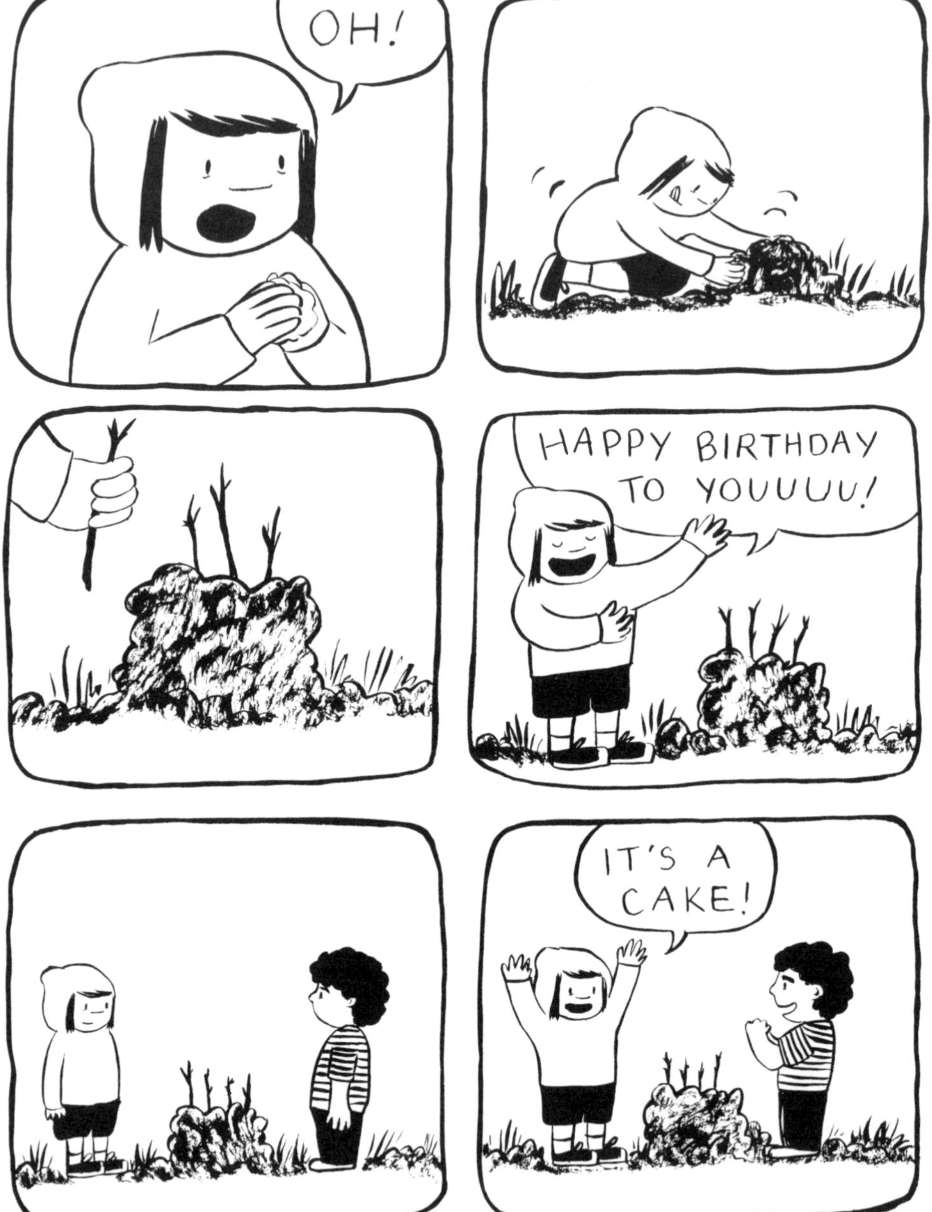
OH!
HAPPY BIRTHDAY TO YOUUUU!
IT'S A CAKE!

MOM

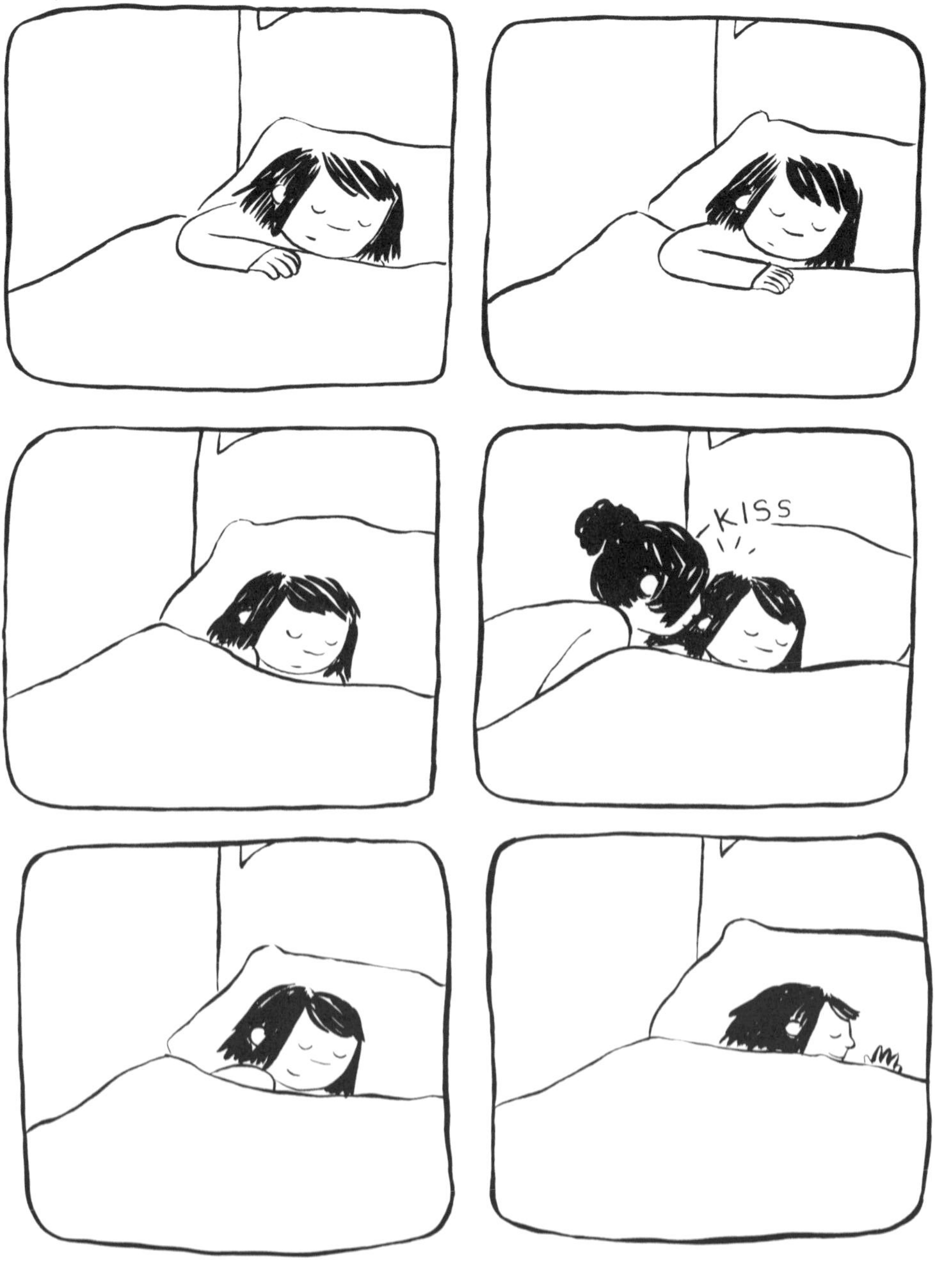
KISS

FRANK

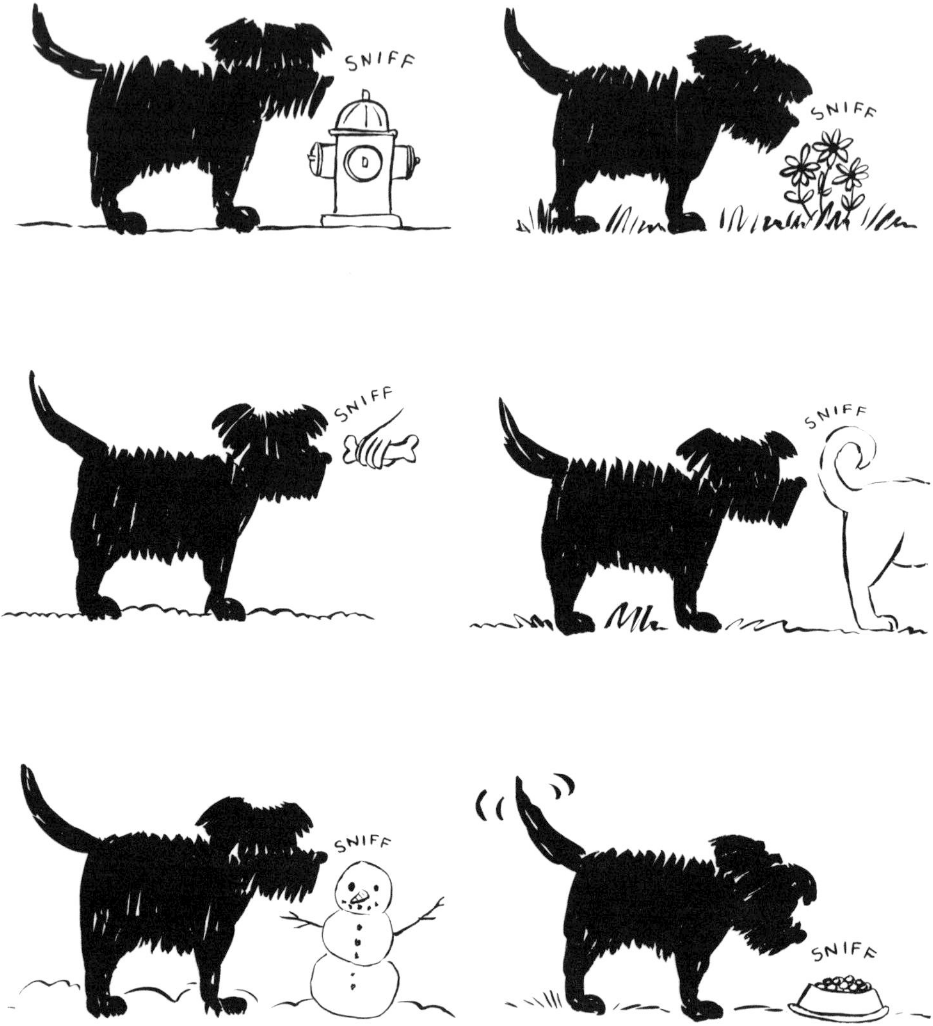
SNIFF
SNIFF
SNIFF
SNIFF
SNIFF
SNIFF

TREASURE

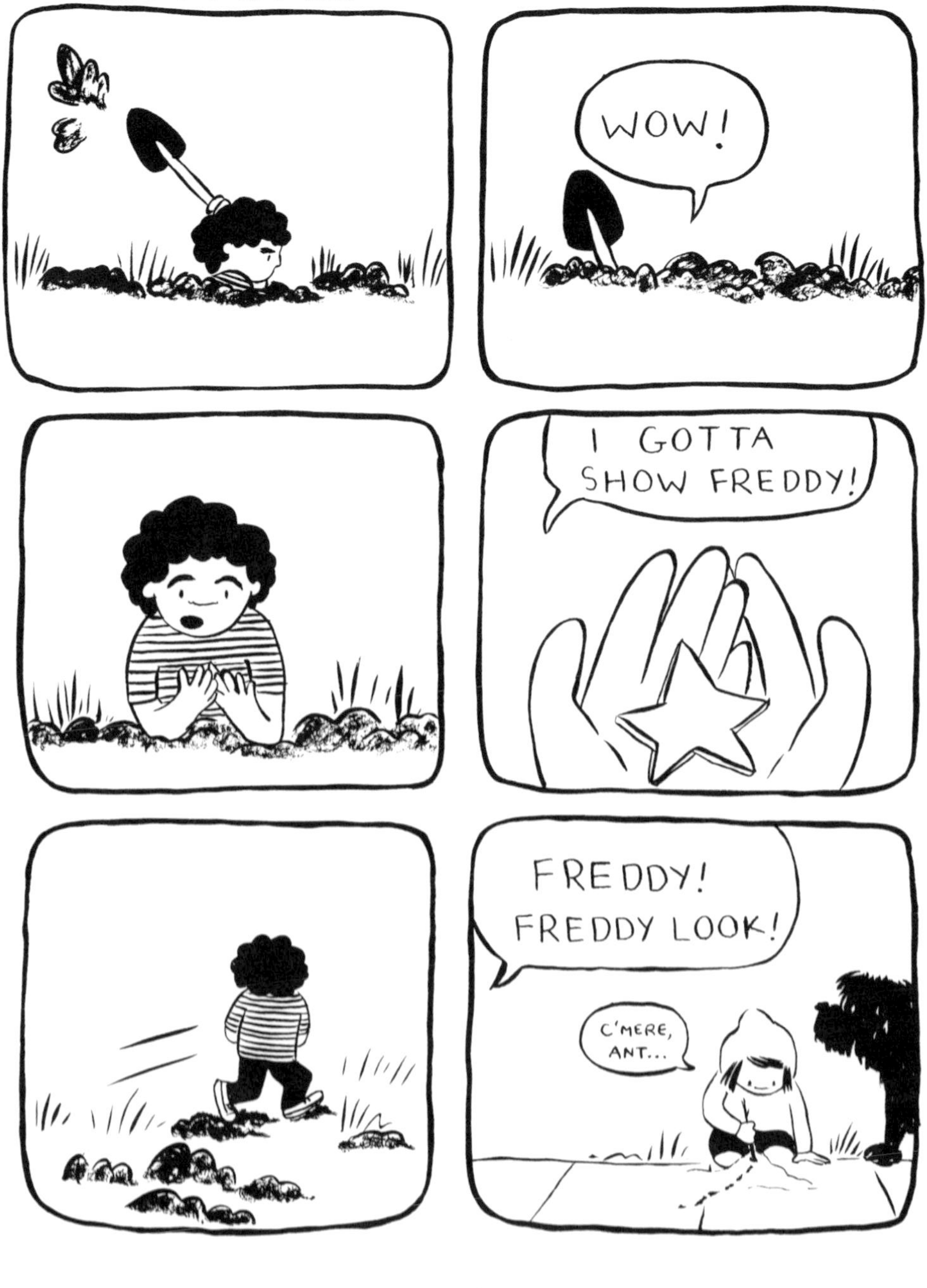
WOW!
I GOTTA SHOW FREDDY!
FREDDY! FREDDY LOOK!
C'MERE, ANT...

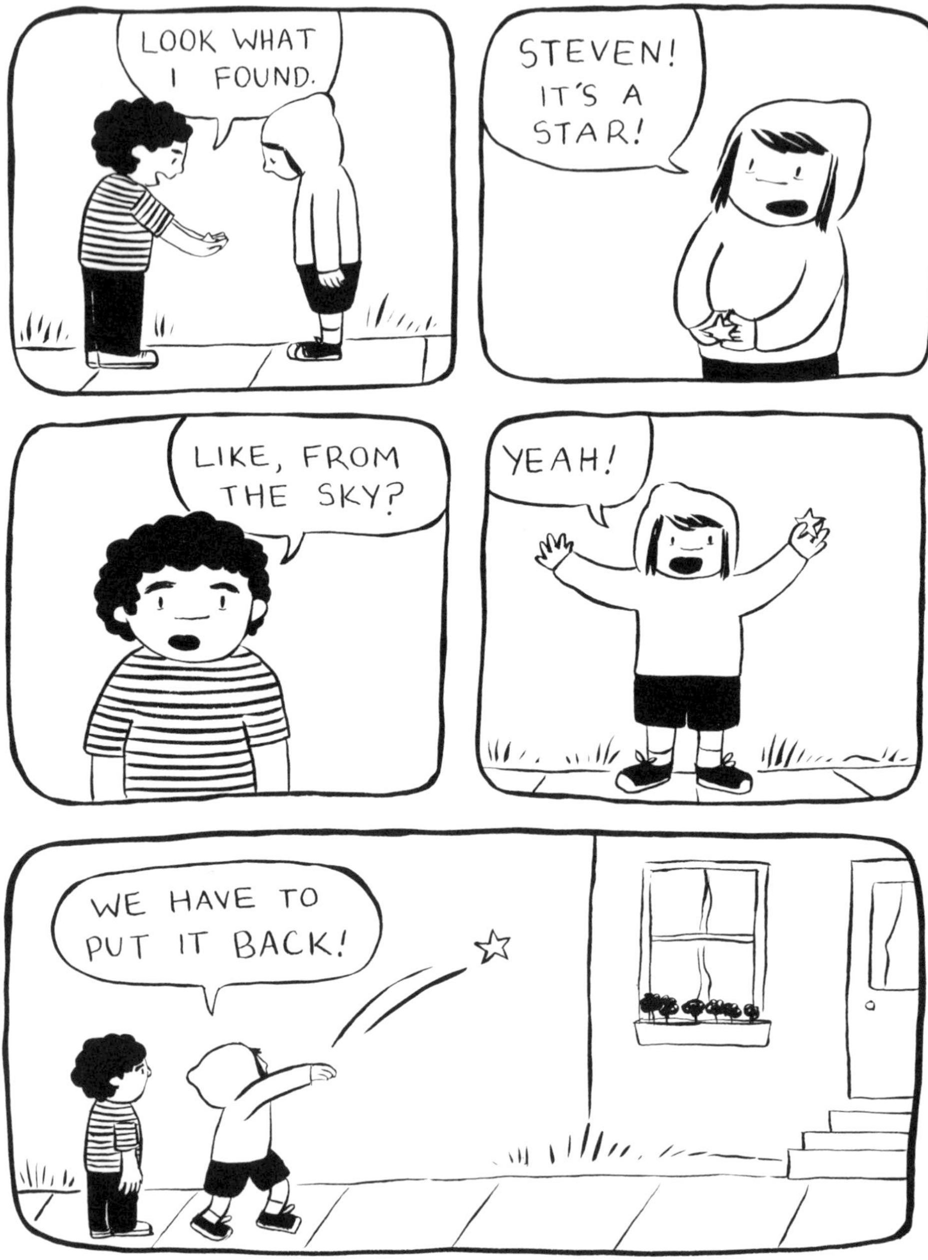
LOOK WHAT I FOUND.
STEVEN! IT'S A STAR!
LIKE, FROM THE SKY?
YEAH!
WE HAVE TO PUT IT BACK!

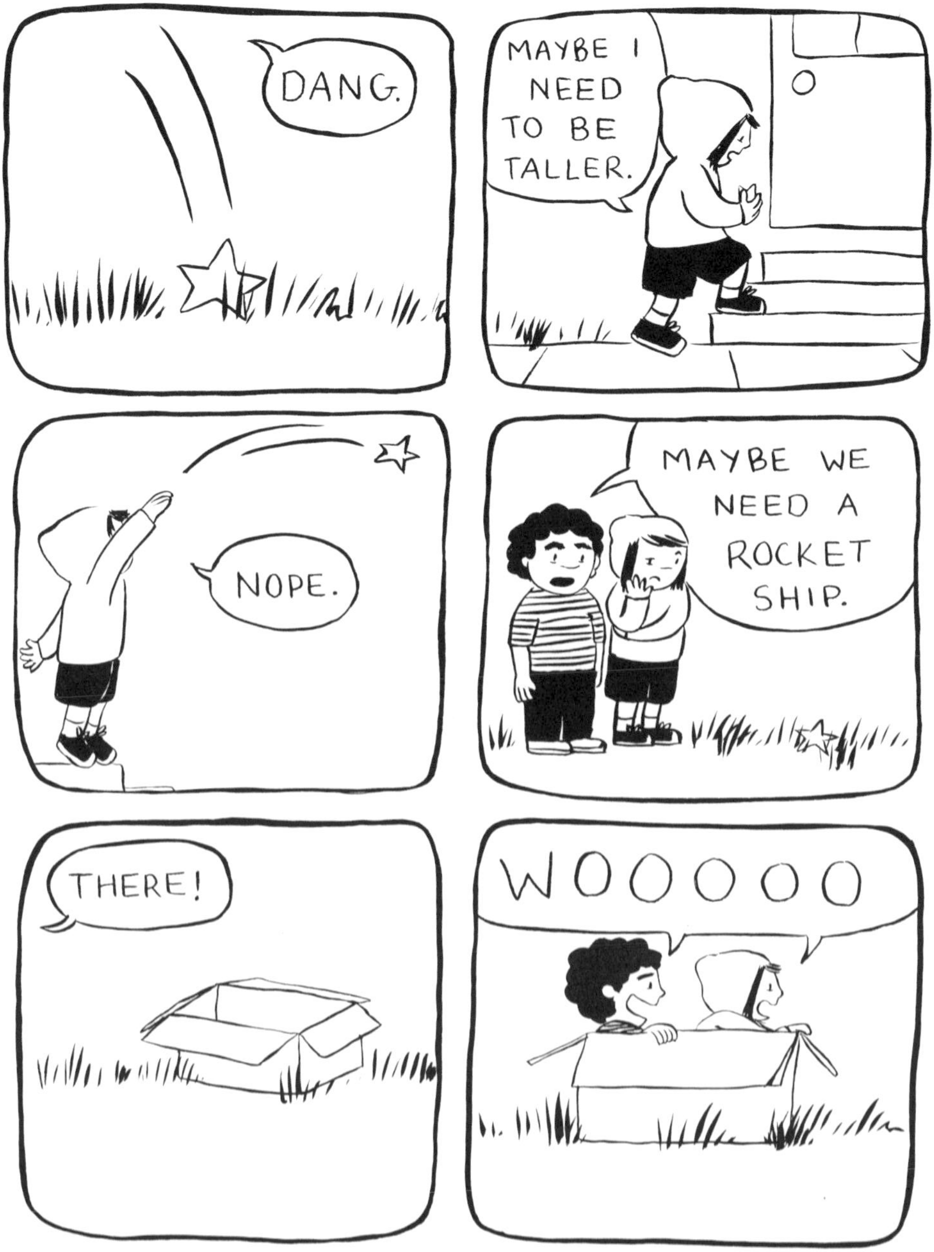

DANG.
MAYBE I NEED TO BE TALLER.
NOPE.
MAYBE WE NEED A ROCKET SHIP.
THERE!
WOOOOO

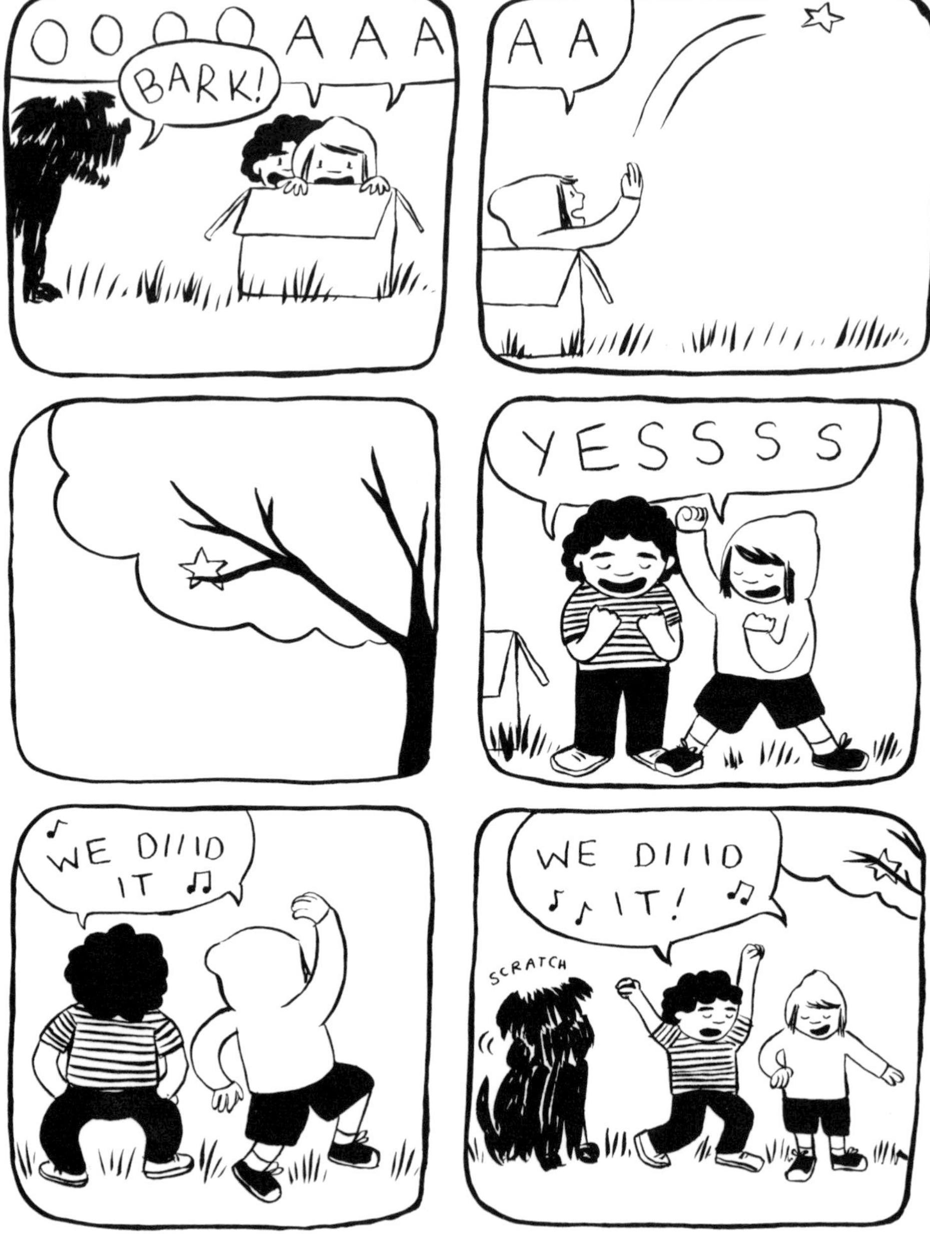
OOOOAAA
BARK!
AA
YESSSS
WE DIIID IT
WE DIIID IT!
SCRATCH

MRS. MEDEIROS

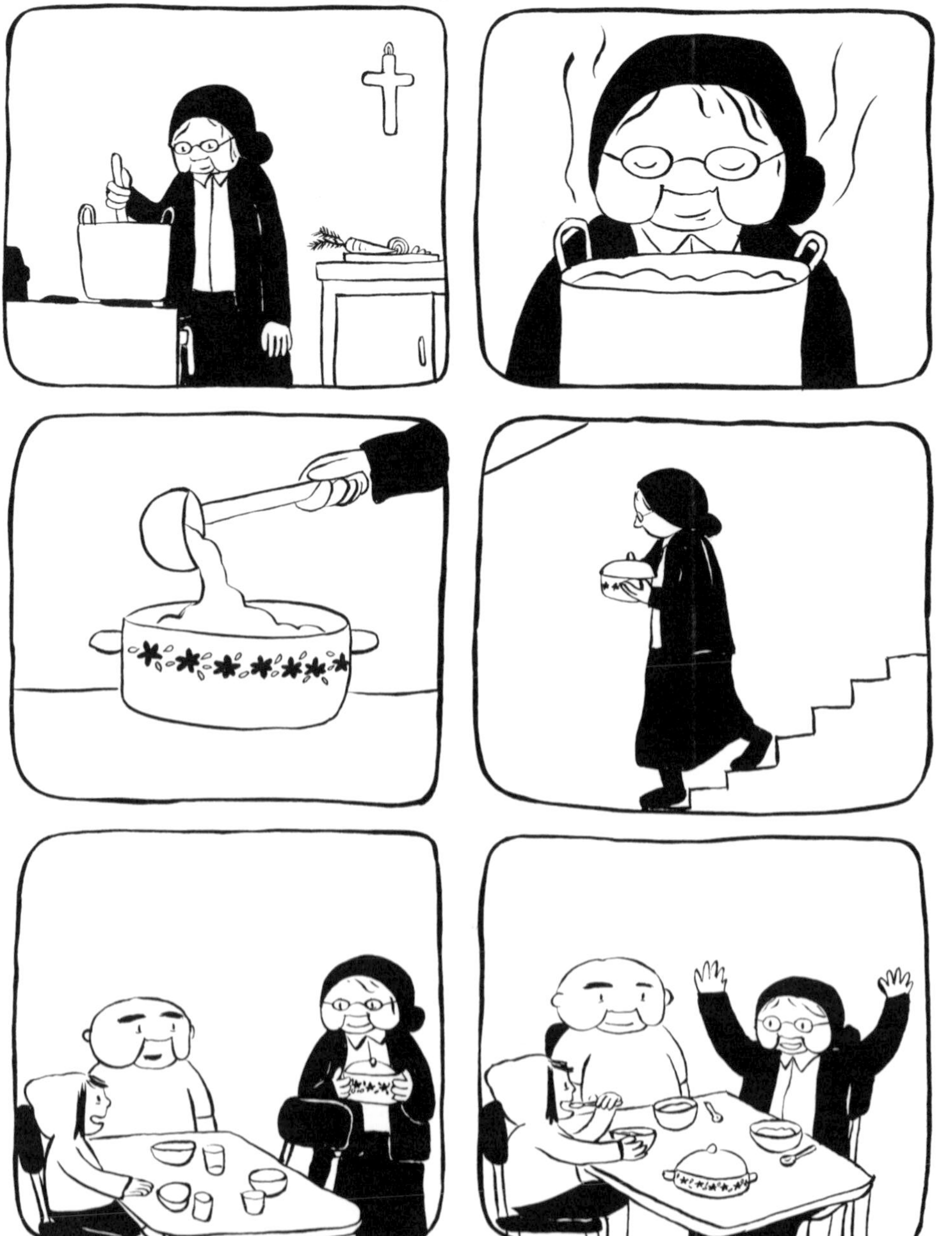

PIZZA NIGHT

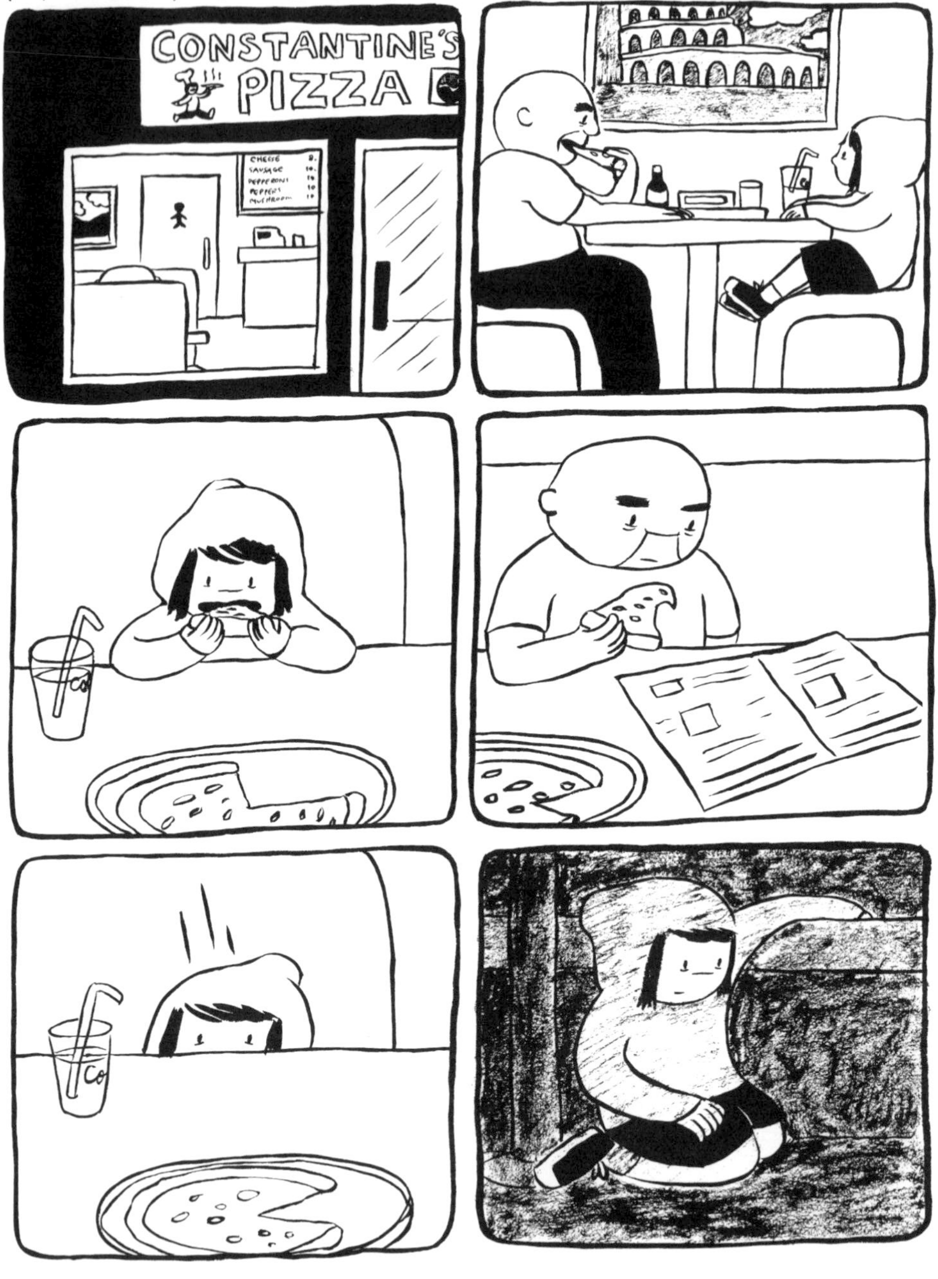

CONSTANTINE'S
PIZZA
CHEESE
SAUSAGE
PEPPERONI
PEPPERS
MUSHROOM

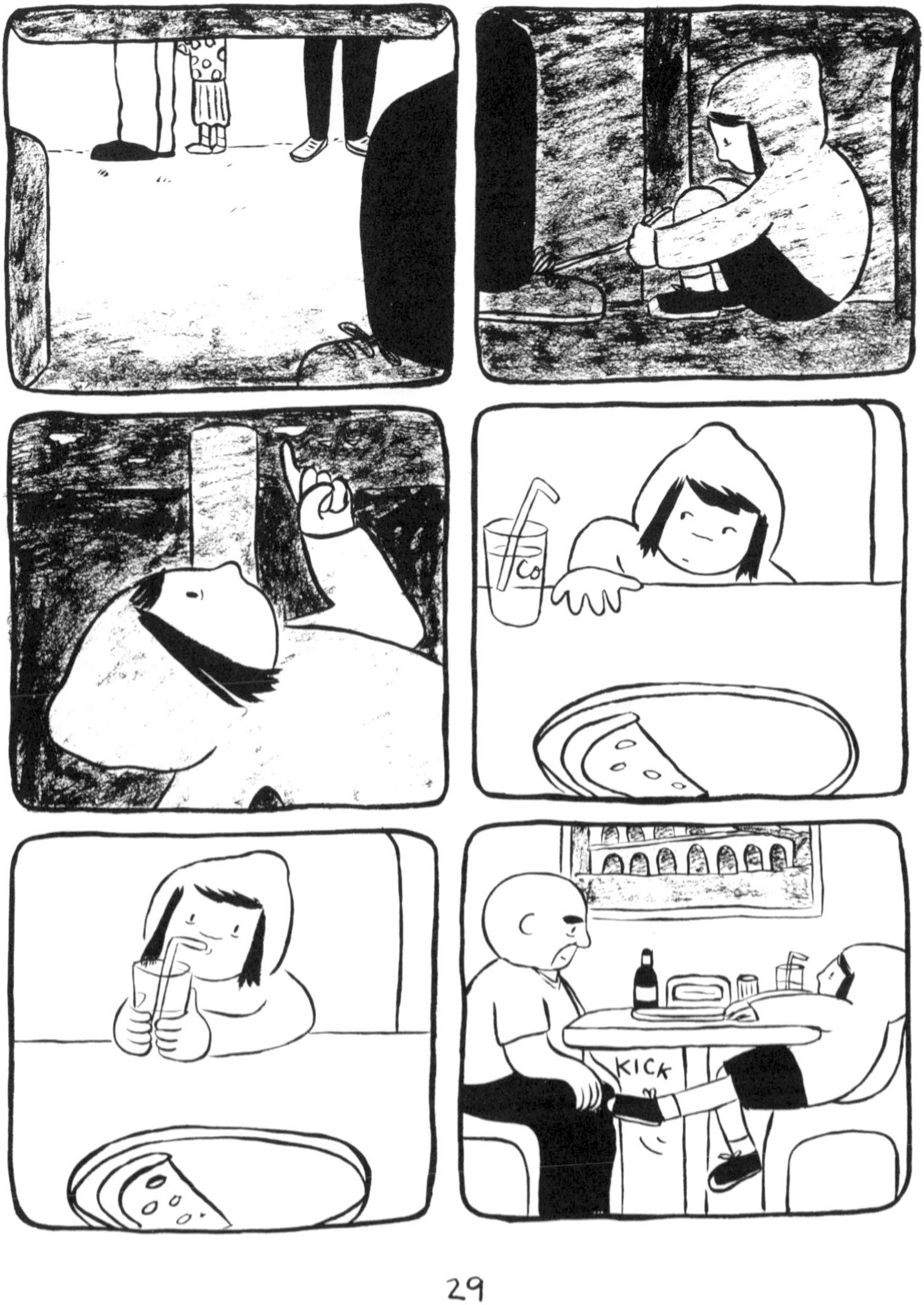
Co
KICK

FLOUR

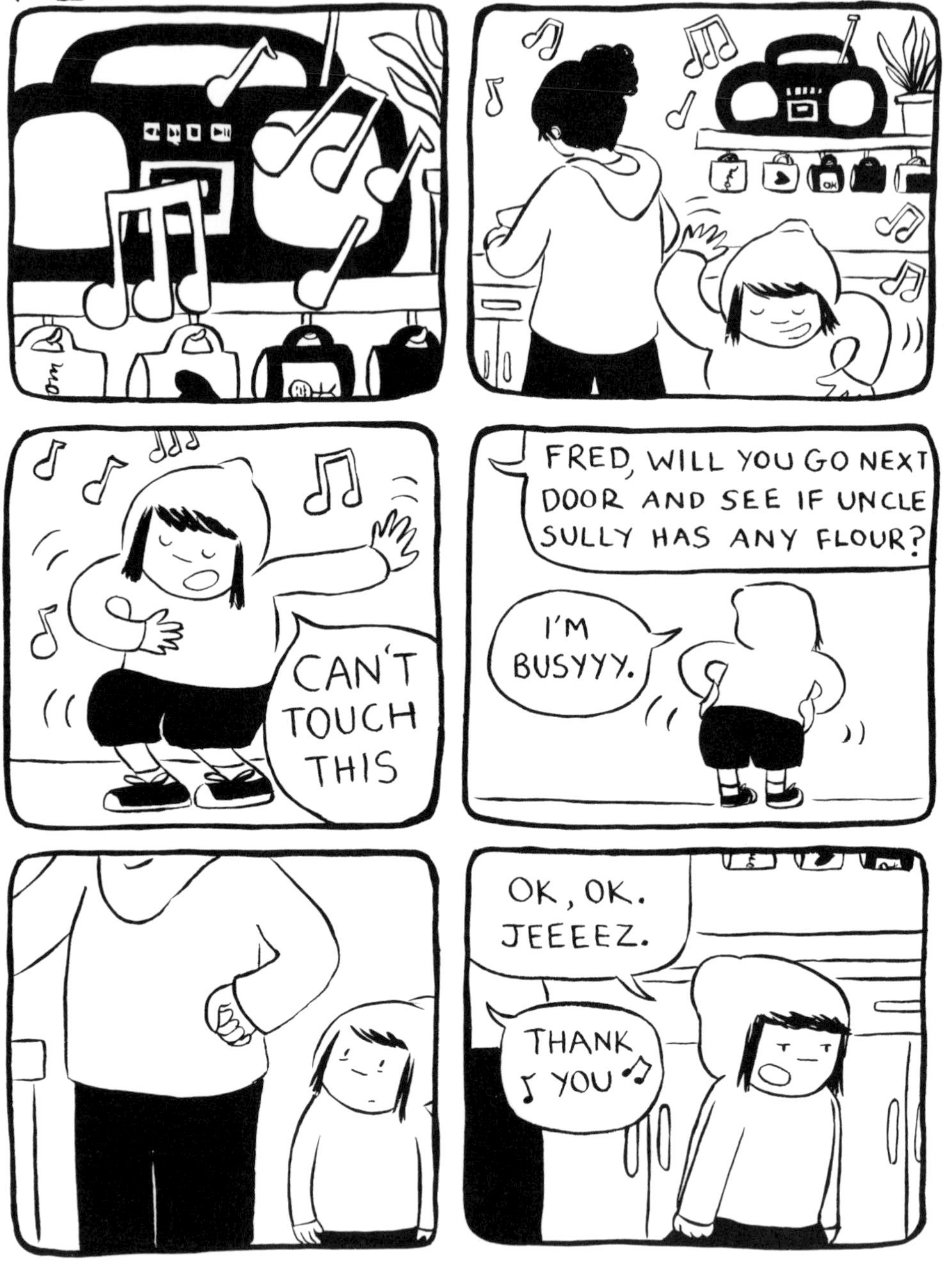
CAN'T TOUCH THIS
FRED, WILL YOU GO NEXT DOOR AND SEE IF UNCLE SULLY HAS ANY FLOUR?
I'M BUSYYY.
OK, OK. JEEEEZ.
THANK YOU

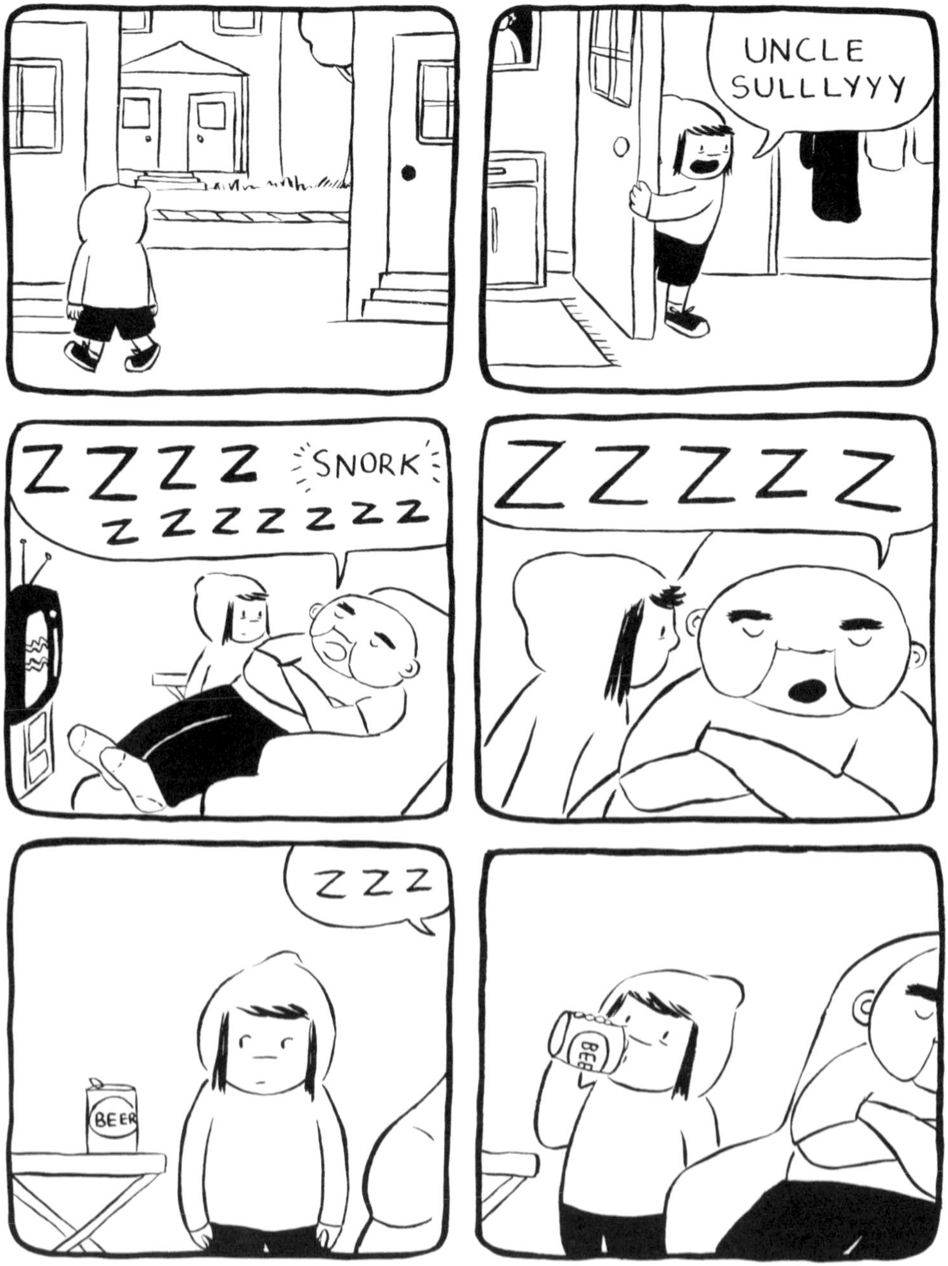
UNCLE SULLLYYY
ZZZZ
SNORK
ZZZZZZZZ
ZZZZZZ
ZZZ
BEER
BEER

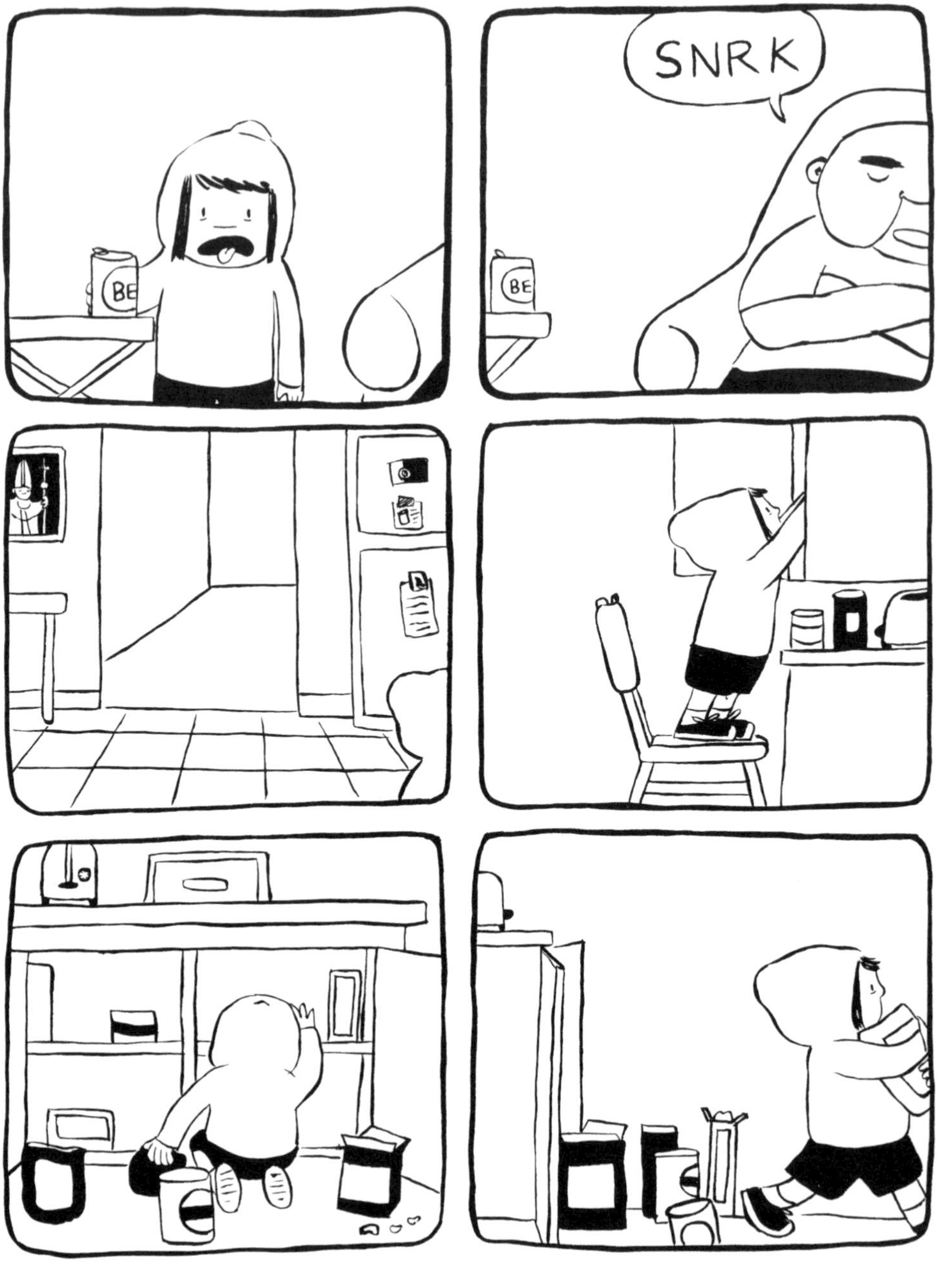
BE
SNRK
BE

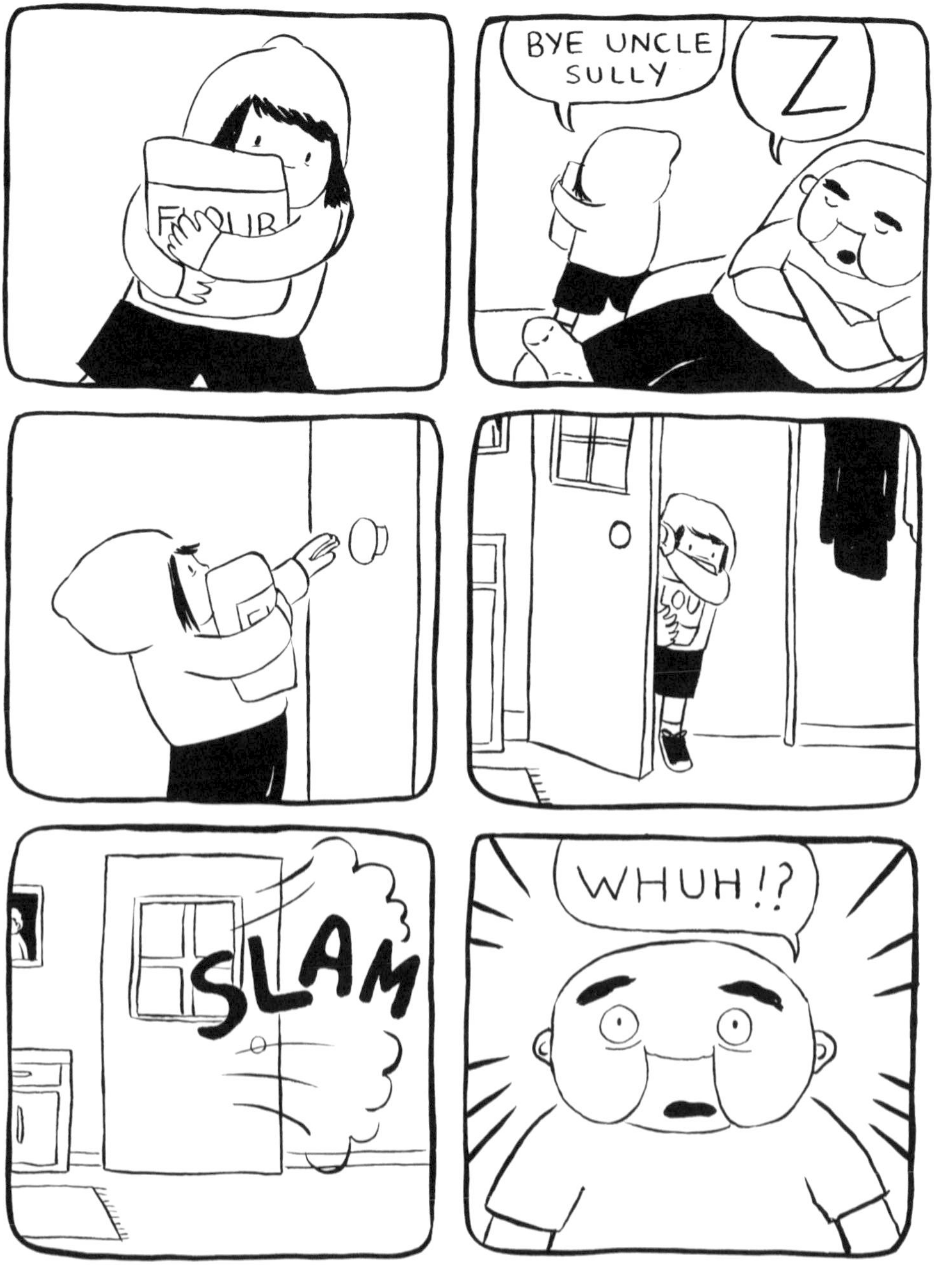
FLOUR
BYE UNCLE SULLY
Z
LOU
SLAM
WHUH!?

POTION

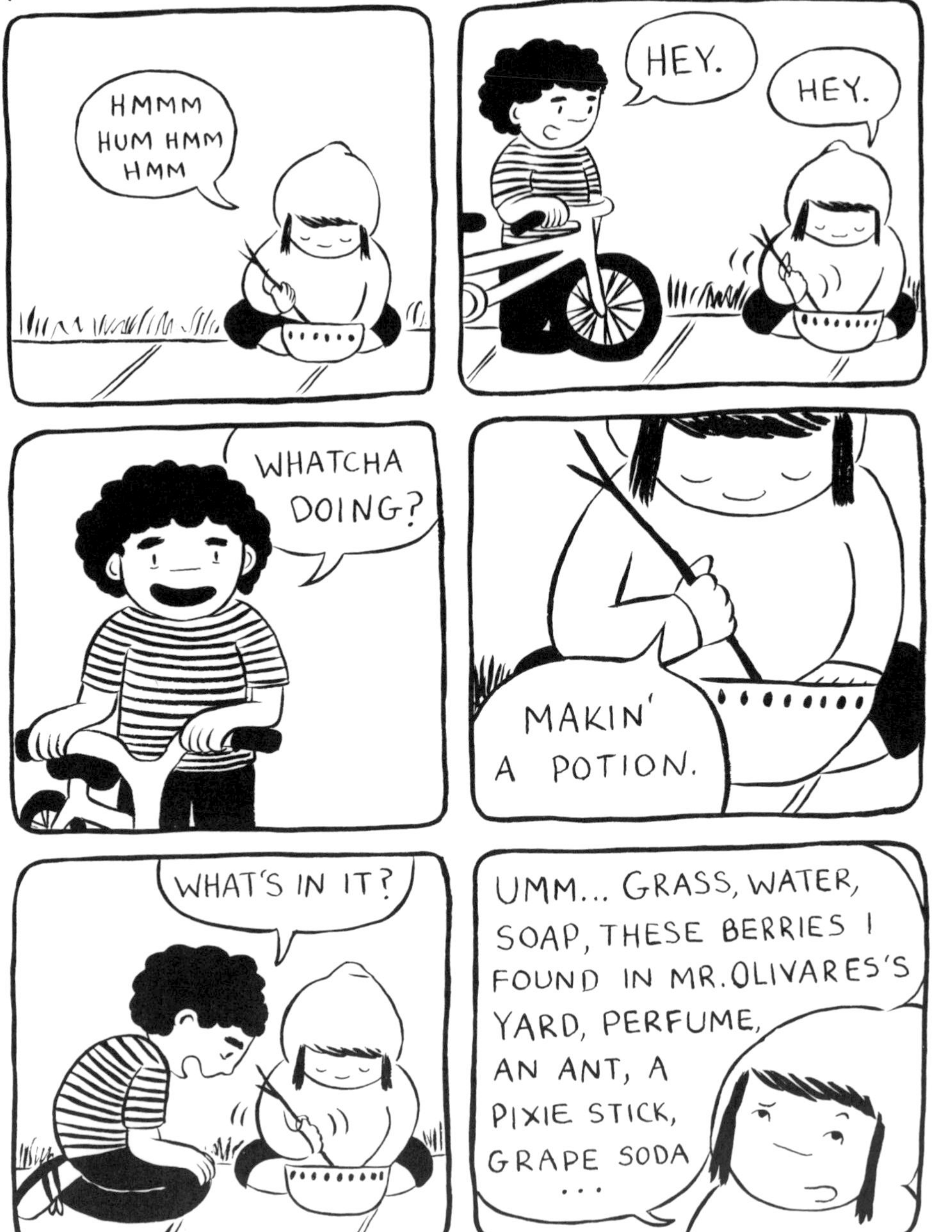
HMMM HUM HMM HMM
HEY.
HEY.
WHATCHA DOING?
MAKIN' A POTION.
WHAT'S IN IT?
UMM... GRASS, WATER, SOAP, THESE BERRIES I FOUND IN MR. OLIVARES'S YARD, PERFUME, AN ANT, A PIXIE STICK, GRAPE SODA ...

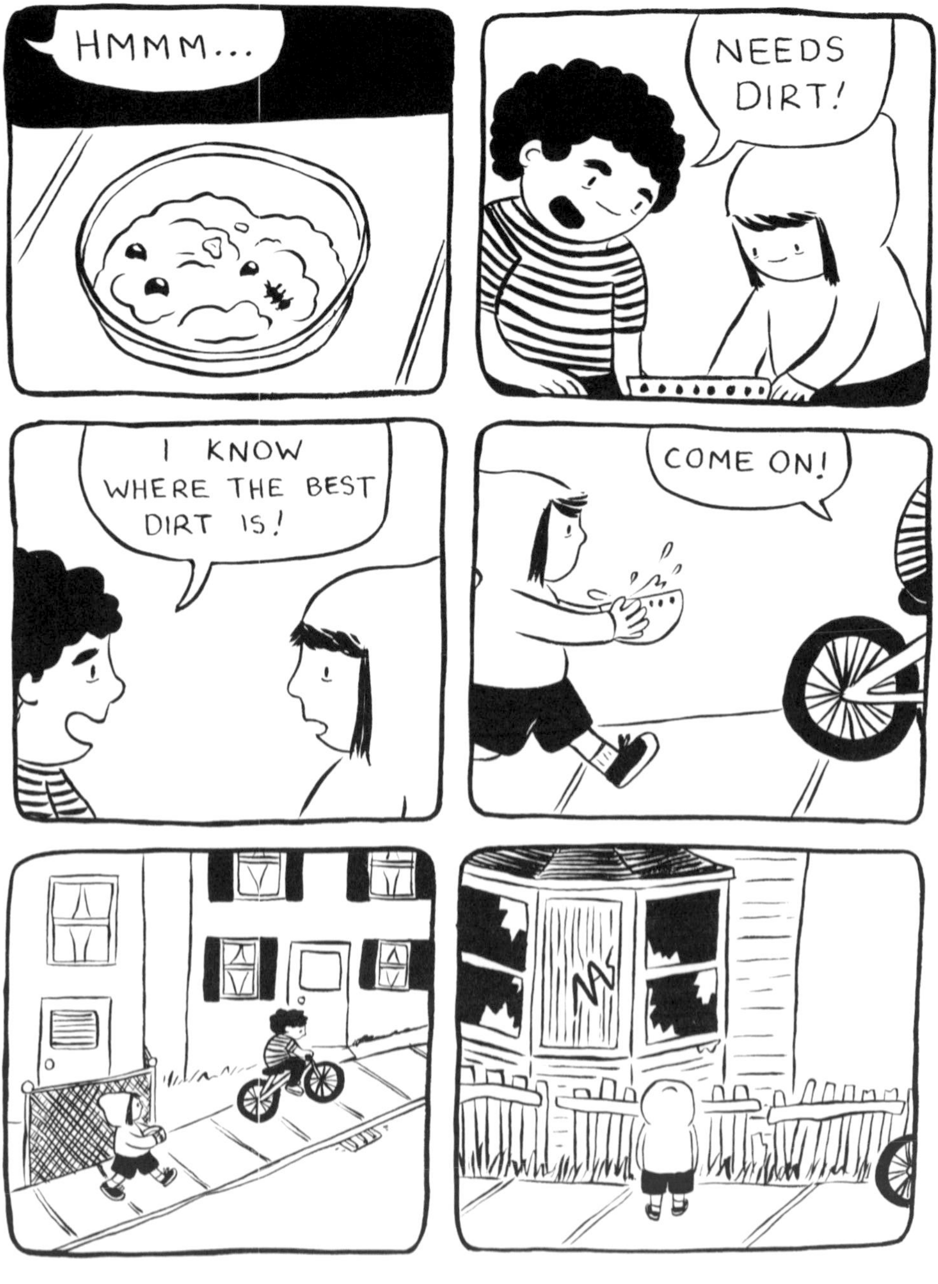

HMMM...
NEEDS DIRT!
I KNOW WHERE THE BEST DIRT IS!
COME ON!

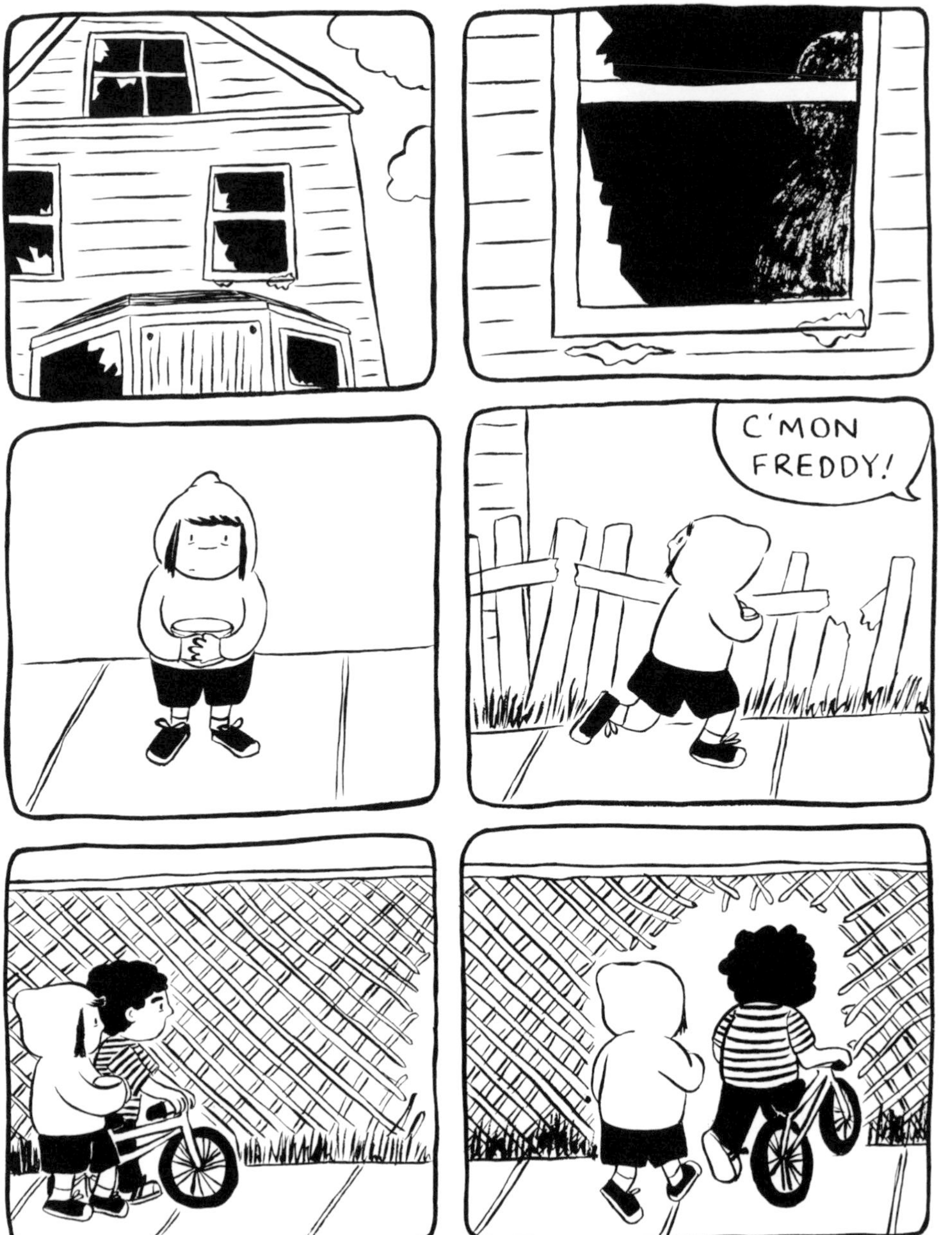
C'MON FREDDY!

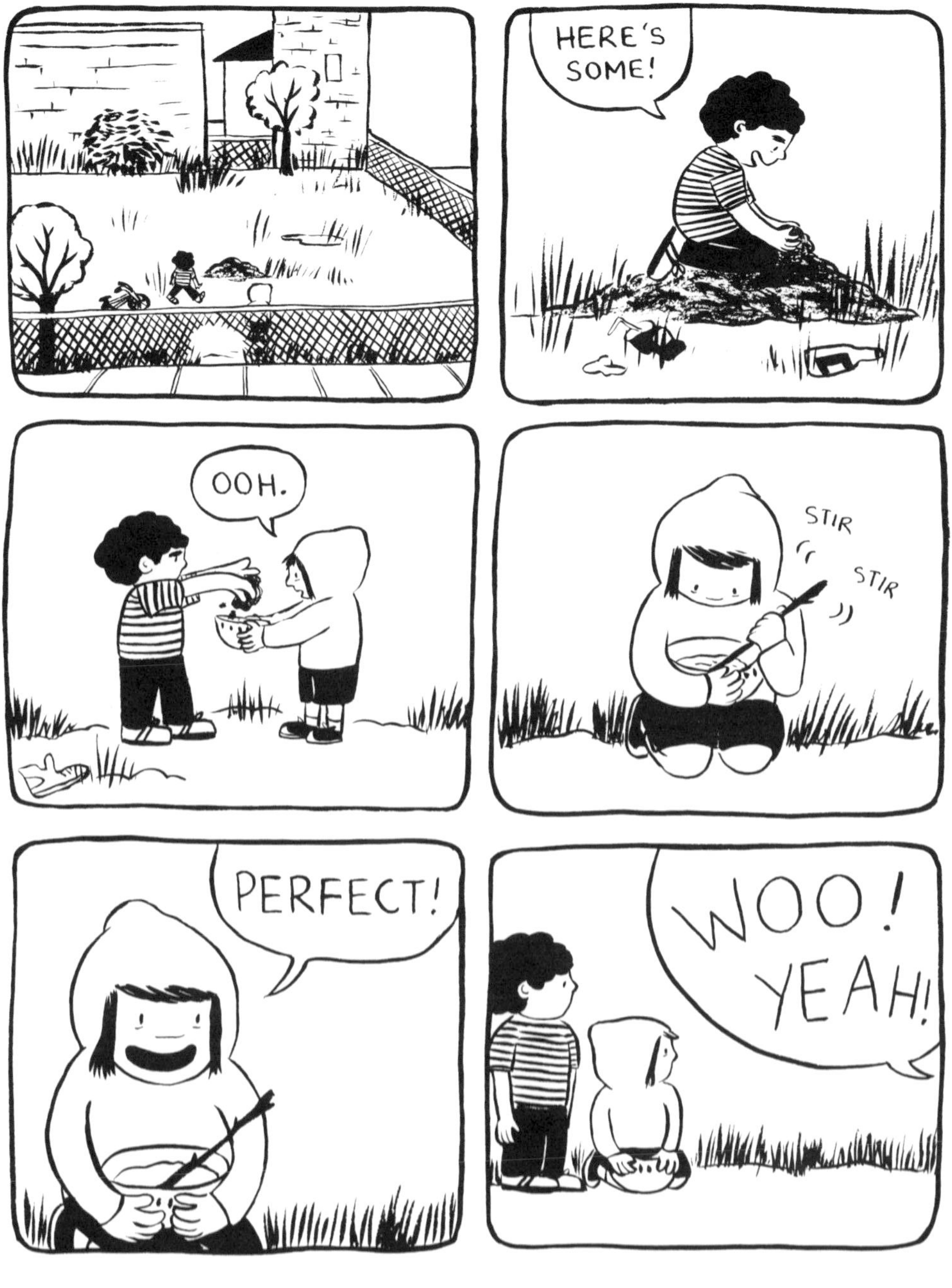
HERE'S SOME!
OOH.
STIR
STIR
PERFECT!
WOO! YEAH!

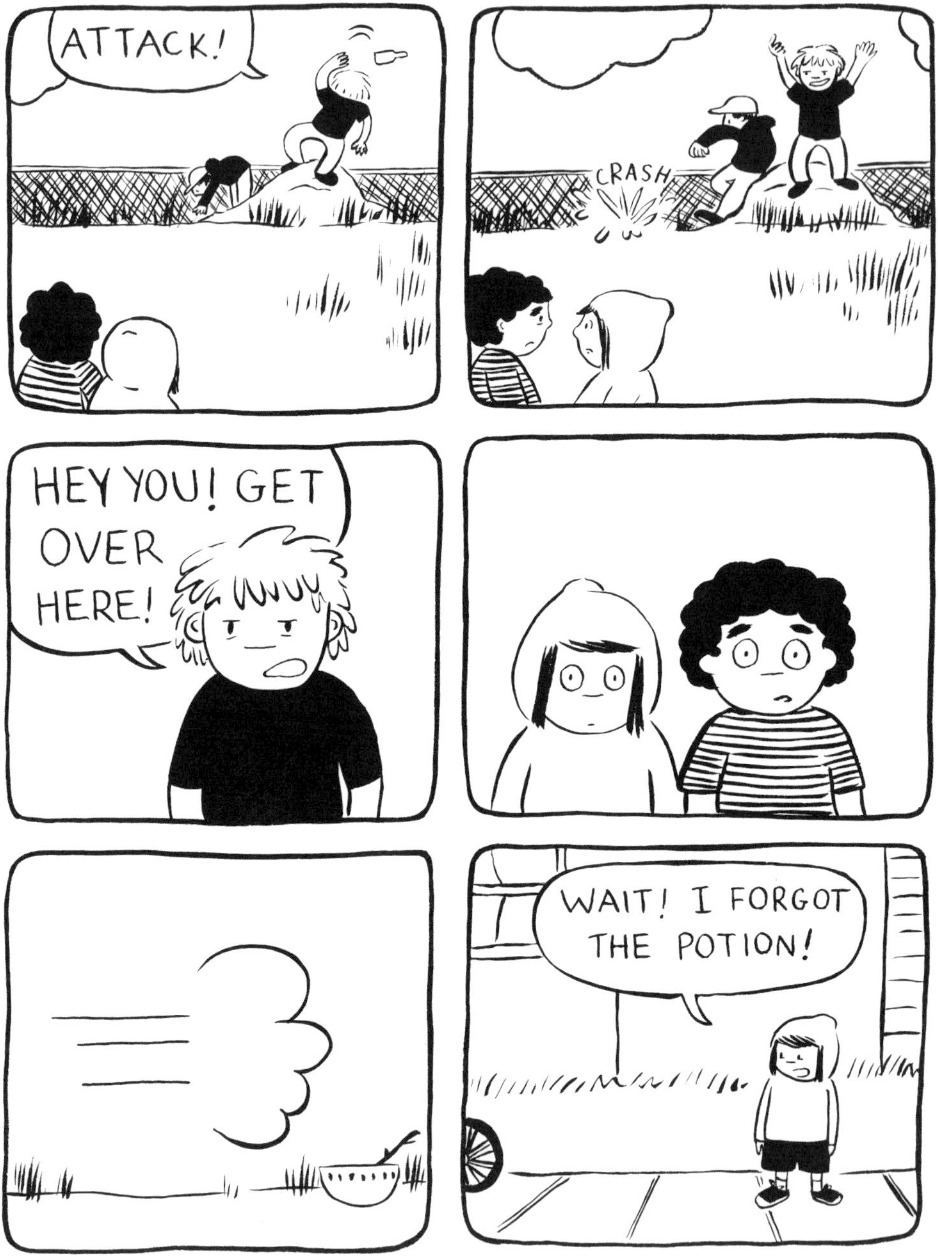
ATTACK!
CRASH
HEY YOU! GET OVER HERE!
WAIT! I FORGOT THE POTION!

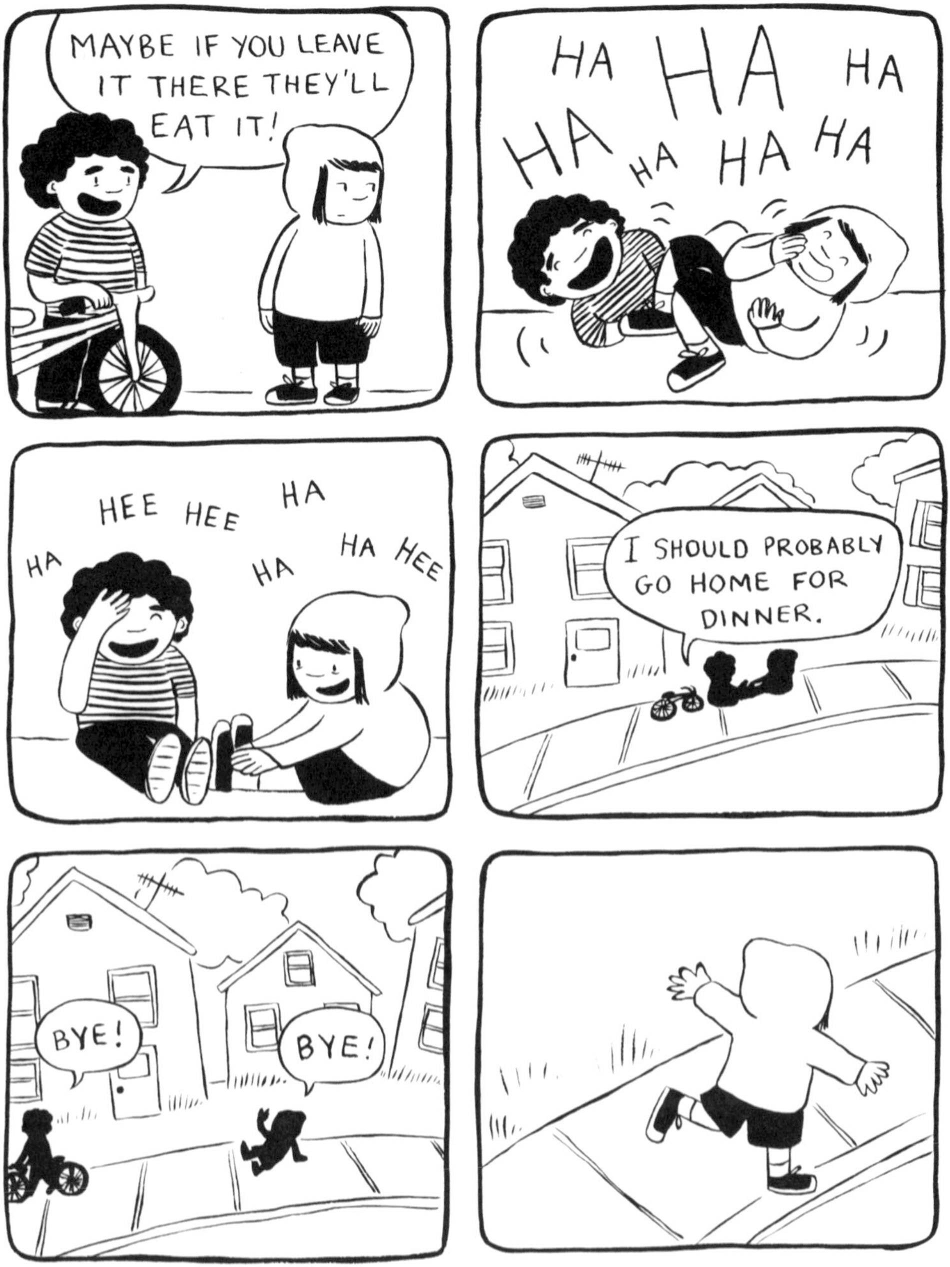
MAYBE IF YOU LEAVE IT THERE THEY'LL EAT IT!
HA HA HA
HA HA HA HA
HEE HEE HA
HA HA HA HEE
I SHOULD PROBABLY GO HOME FOR DINNER.
BYE!
BYE!

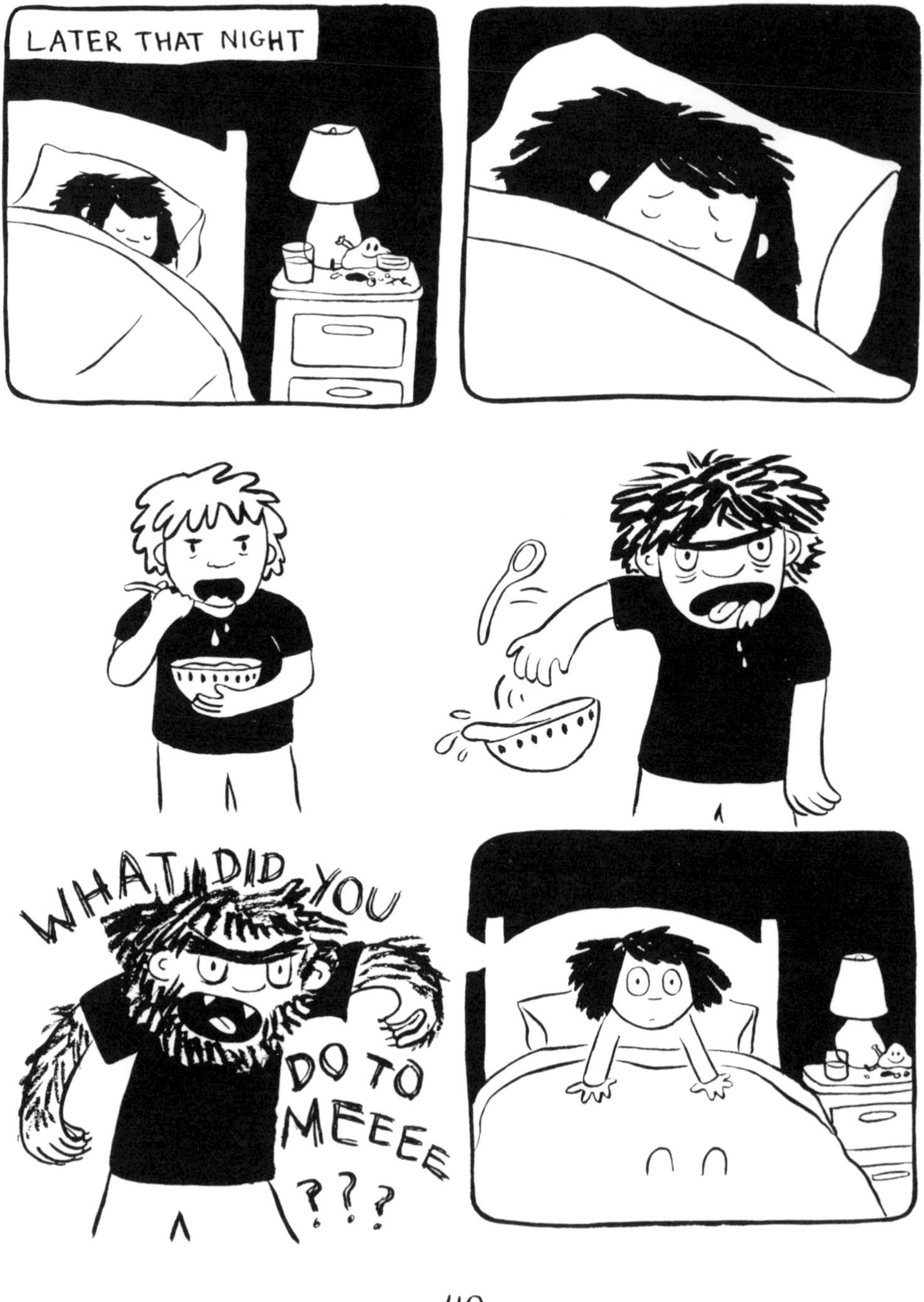
LATER THAT NIGHT
WHAT DID YOU
DO TO
MEEEE
???

SCHOOL

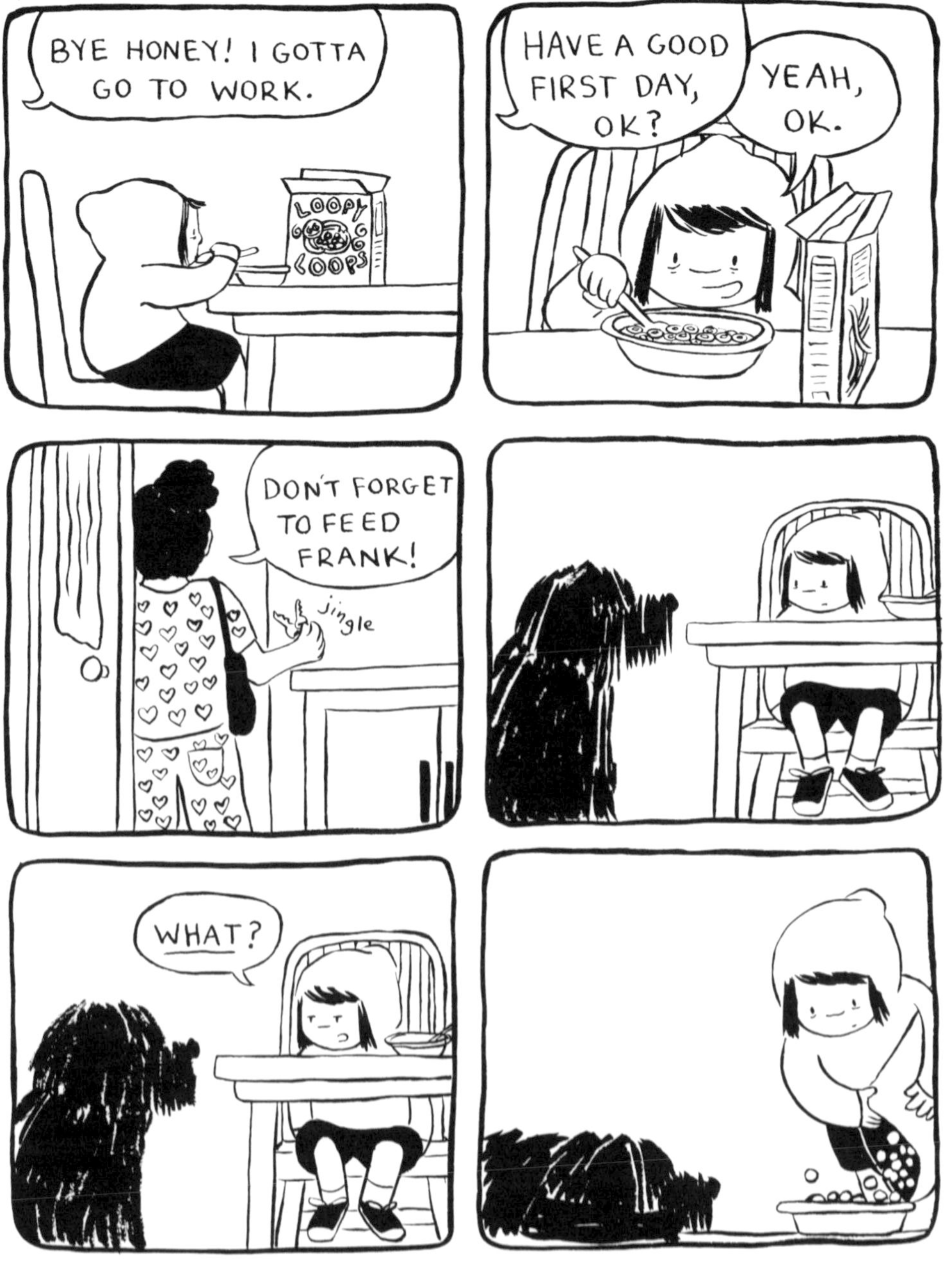
BYE HONEY! I GOTTA GO TO WORK.
LOOPY LOOPS
HAVE A GOOD FIRST DAY, OK?
YEAH, OK.
DON'T FORGET TO FEED FRANK!
jingle
WHAT?

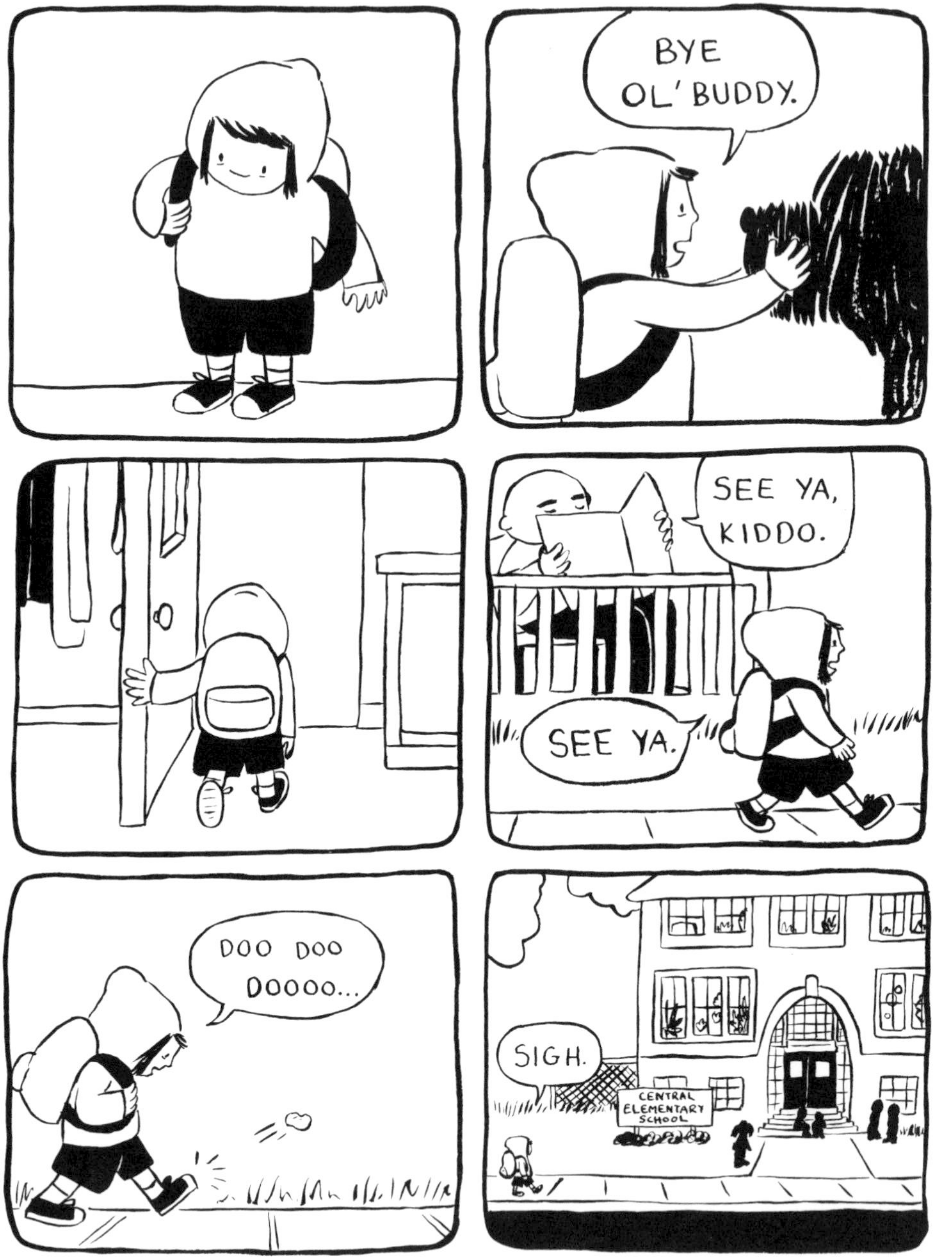
BYE OL' BUDDY.
SEE YA, KIDDO.
SEE YA.
DOO DOO DOOOO...
SIGH.
CENTRAL ELEMENTARY SCHOOL

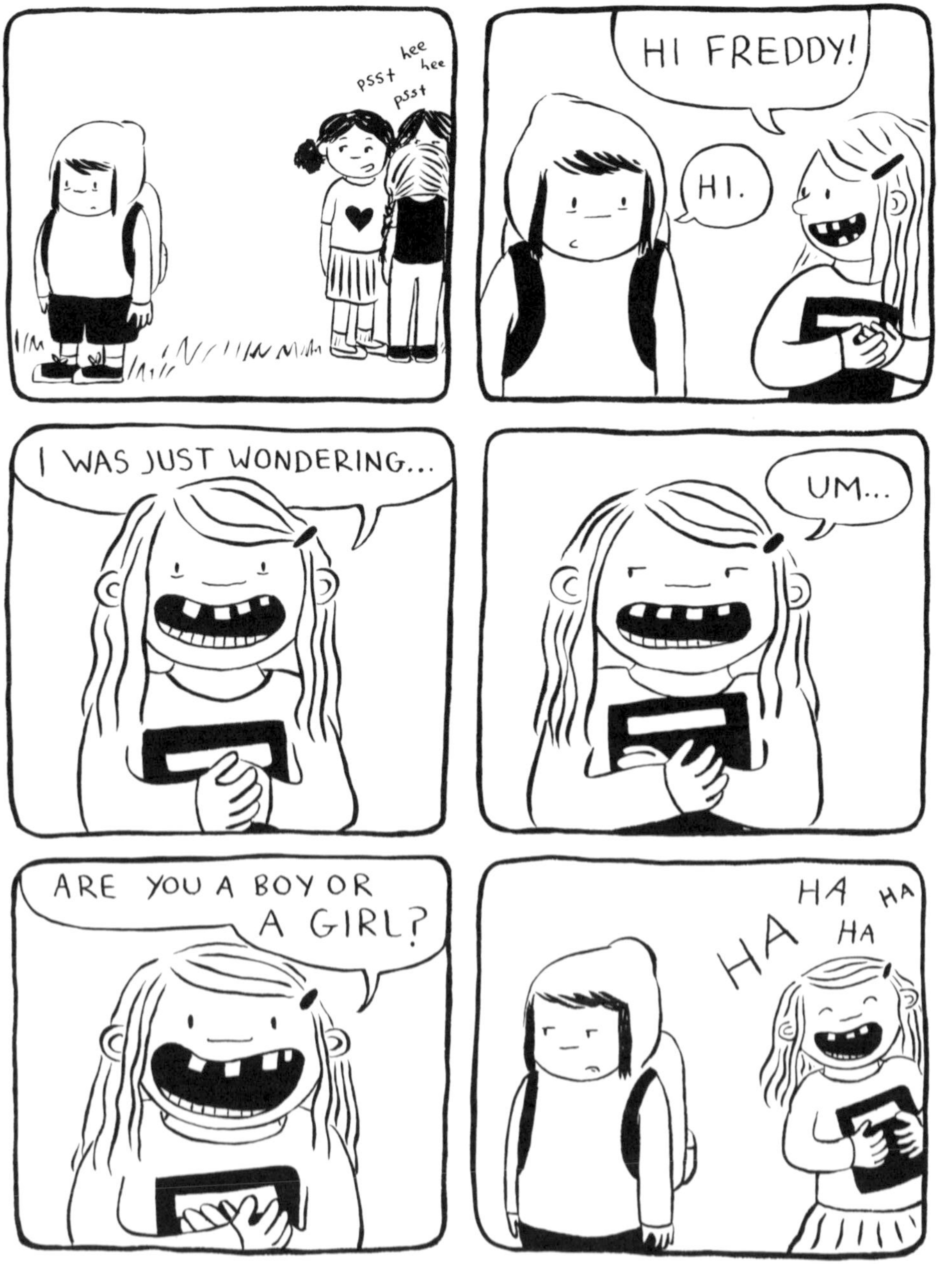
pssst
hee
hee
psst
HI FREDDY!
HI.
I WAS JUST WONDERING...
UM...
ARE YOU A BOY OR A GIRL?
HA
HA
HA
HA

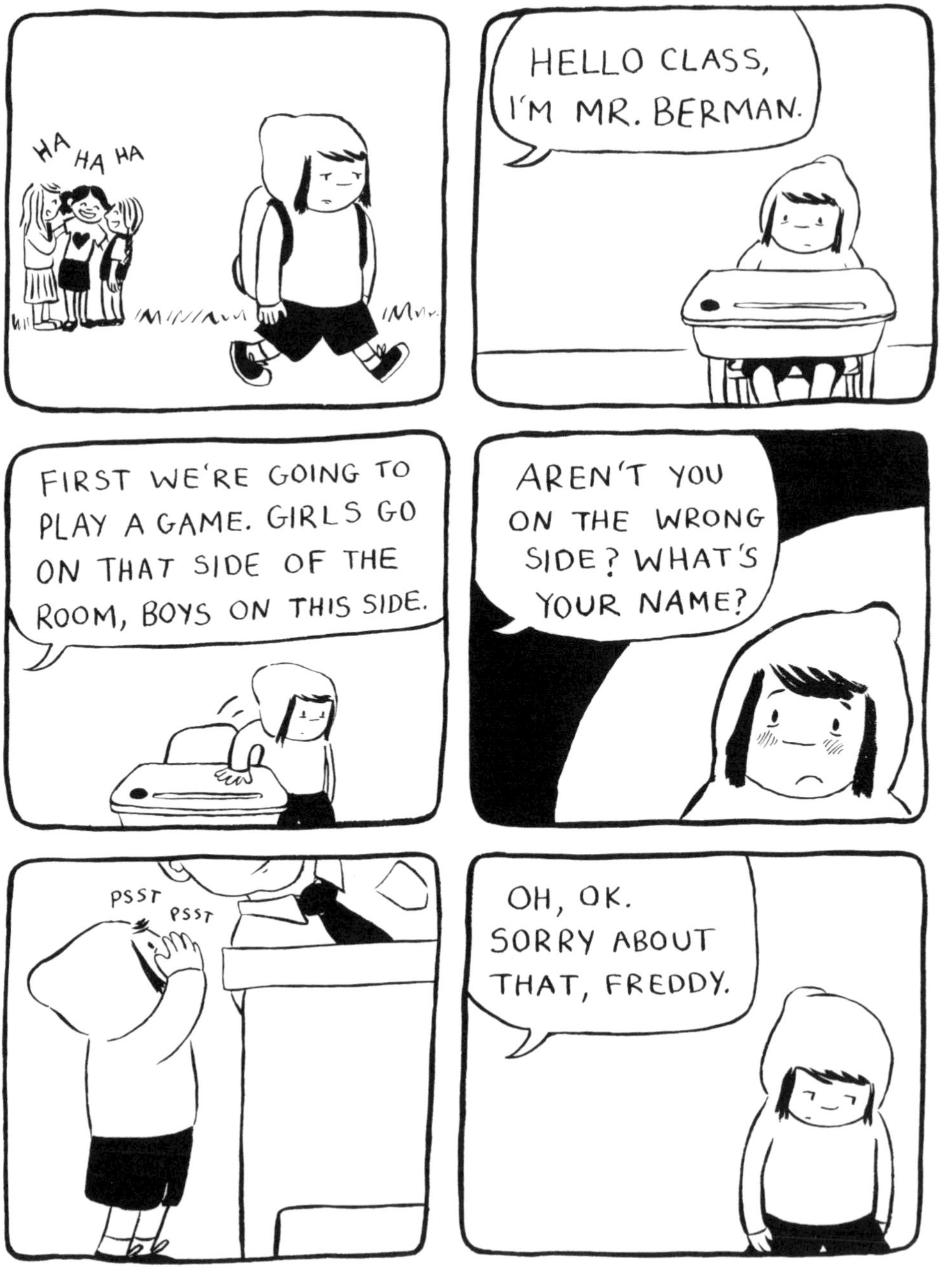
HA HA HA
HELLO CLASS, I'M MR. BERMAN.
FIRST WE'RE GOING TO PLAY A GAME. GIRLS GO ON THAT SIDE OF THE ROOM, BOYS ON THIS SIDE.
AREN'T YOU ON THE WRONG SIDE? WHAT'S YOUR NAME?
PSST PSST
OH, OK. SORRY ABOUT THAT, FREDDY.

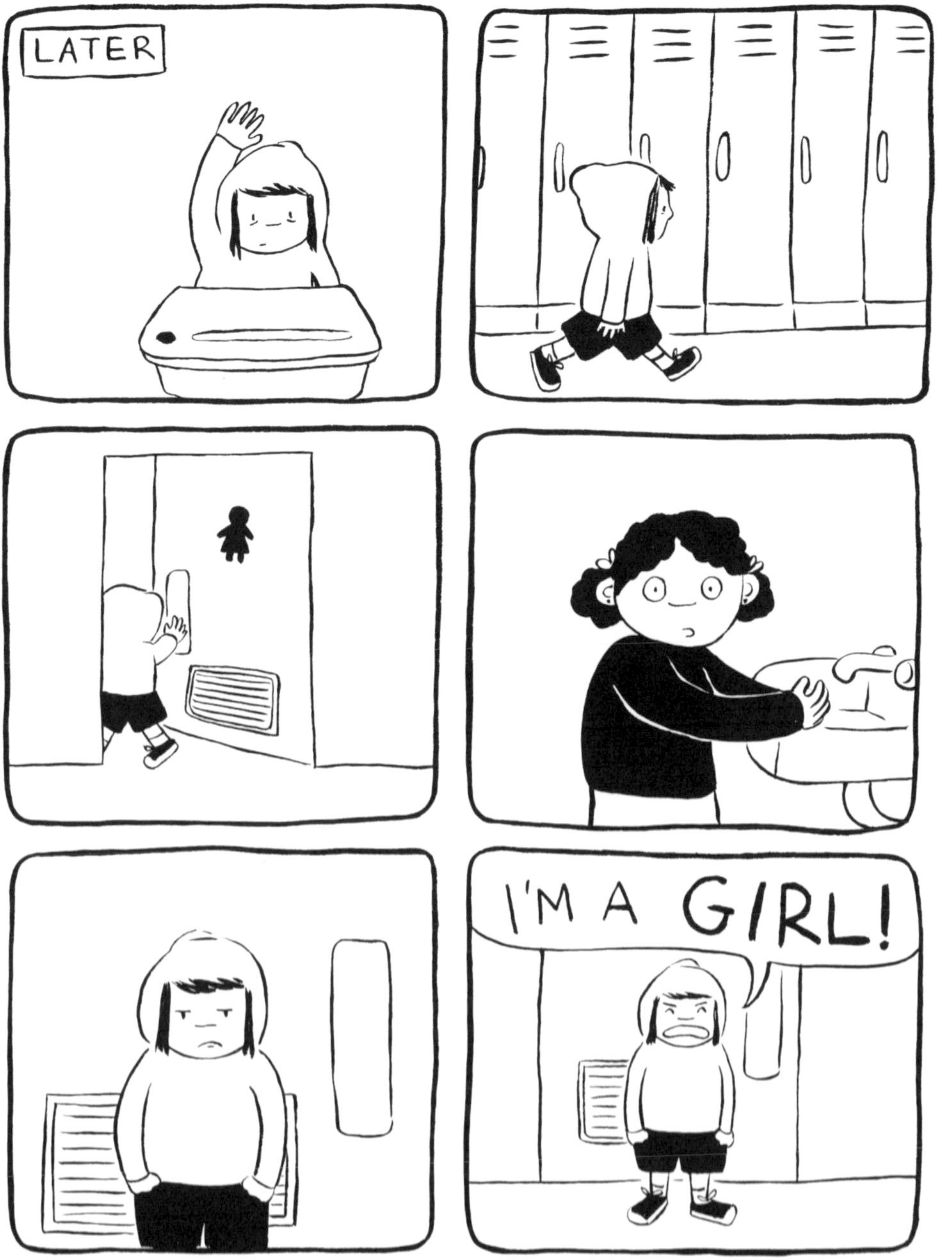
LATER
I'M A GIRL!

THE FAIR

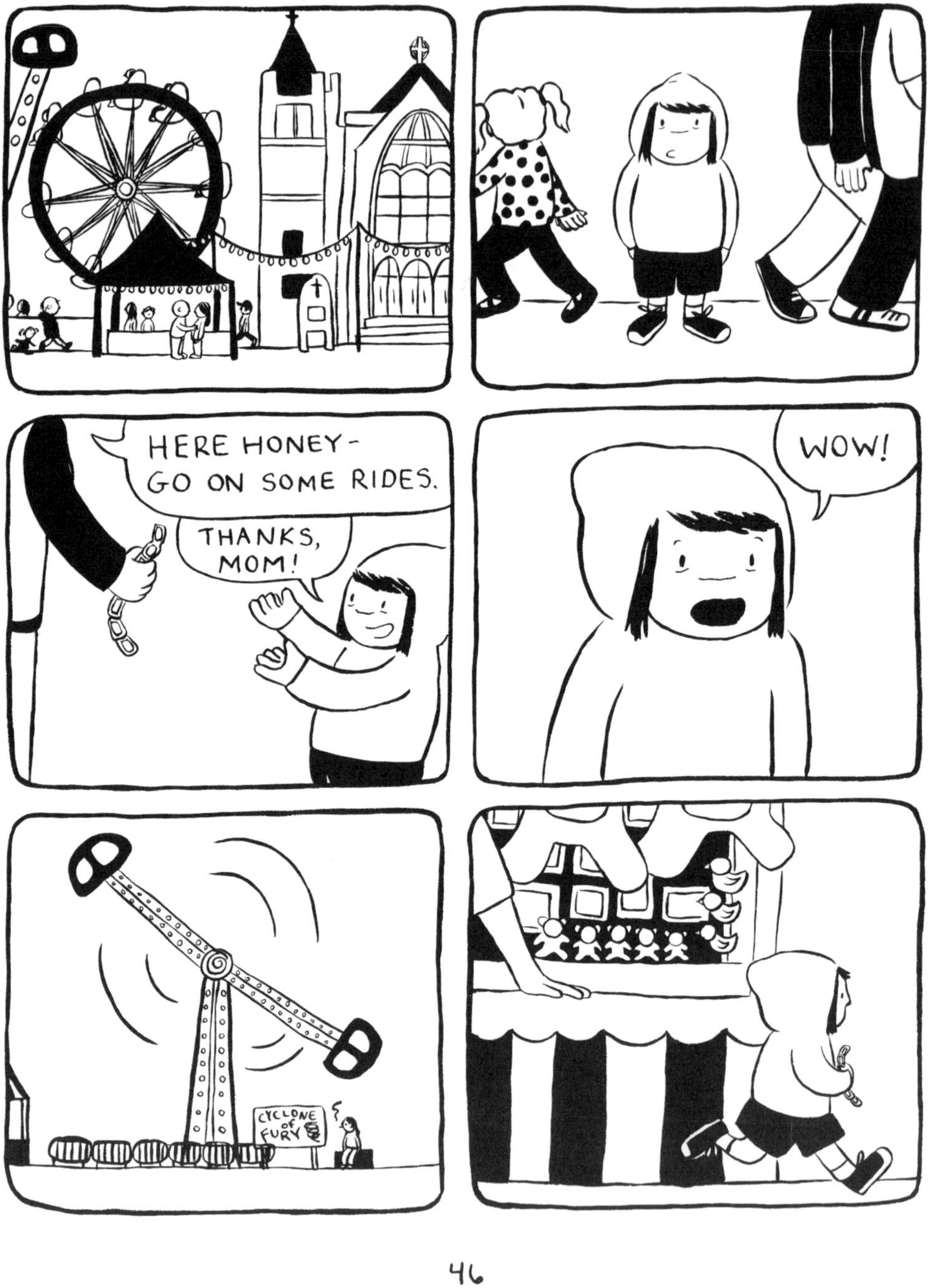
HERE HONEY-
GO ON SOME RIDES.
THANKS,
MOM!
WOW!
CYCLONE of FURY

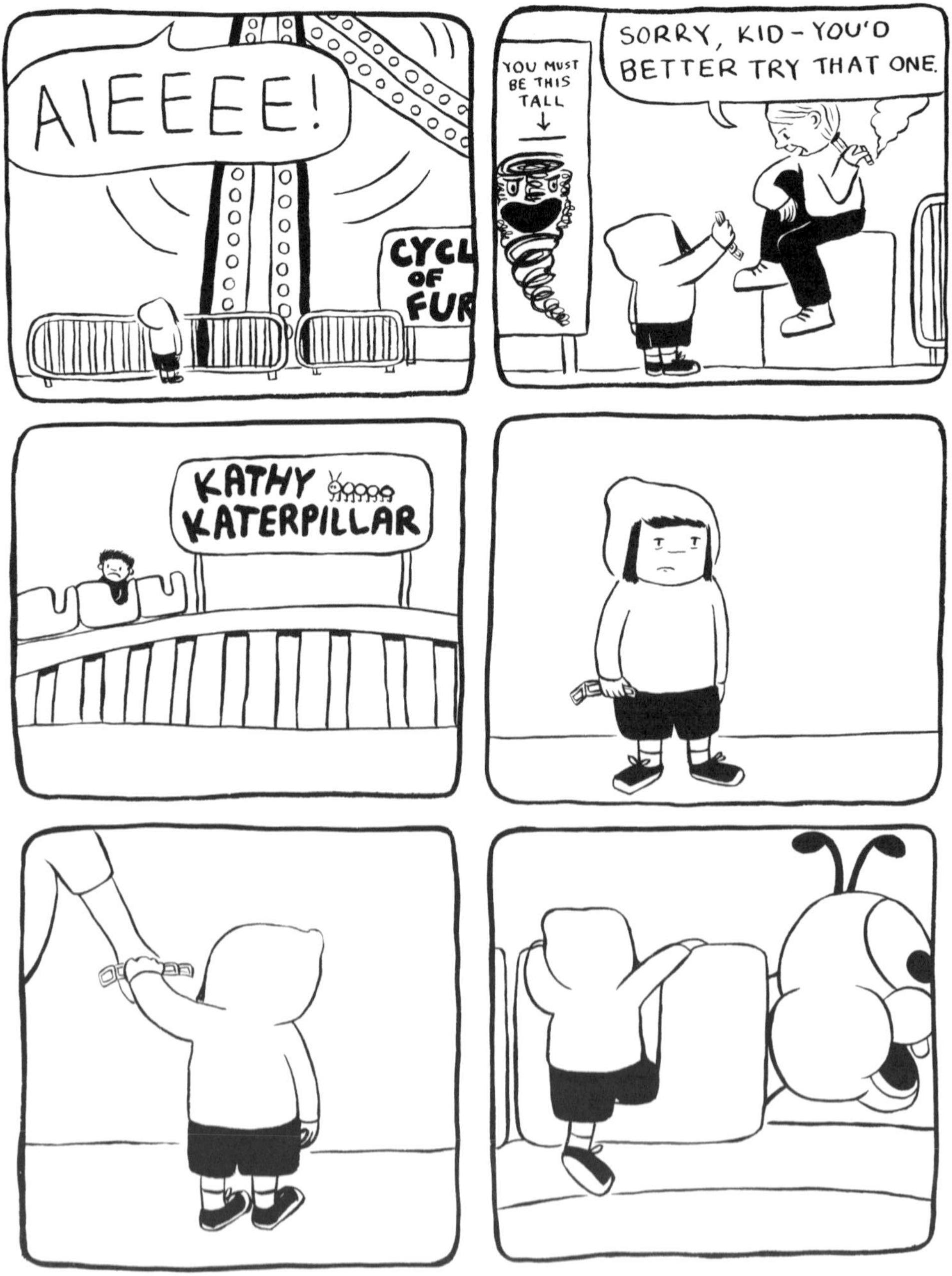
AIEEEE!
CYCL
OF
FUR
YOU MUST BE THIS TALL
SORRY, KID - YOU'D BETTER TRY THAT ONE.
KATHY KATERPILLAR

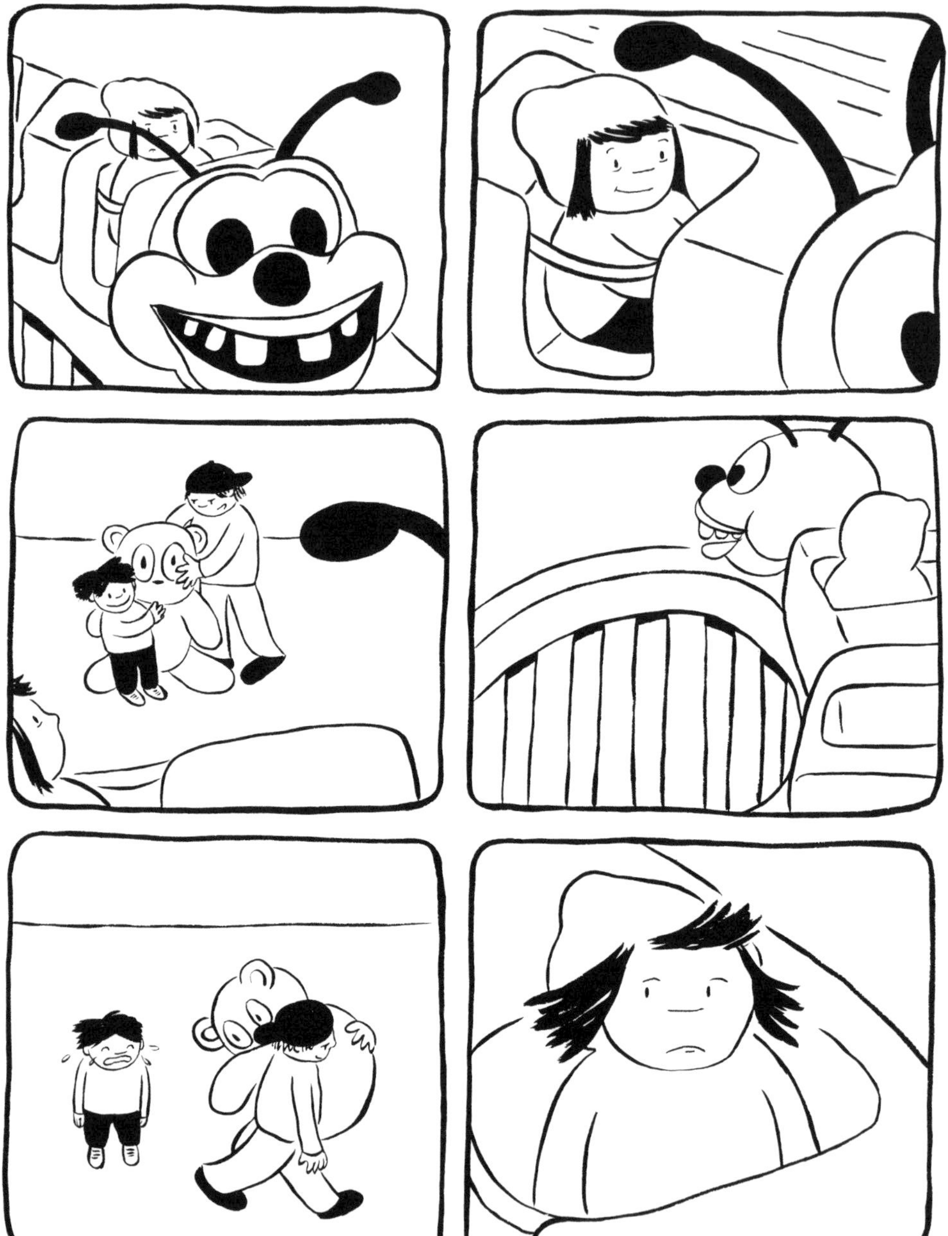

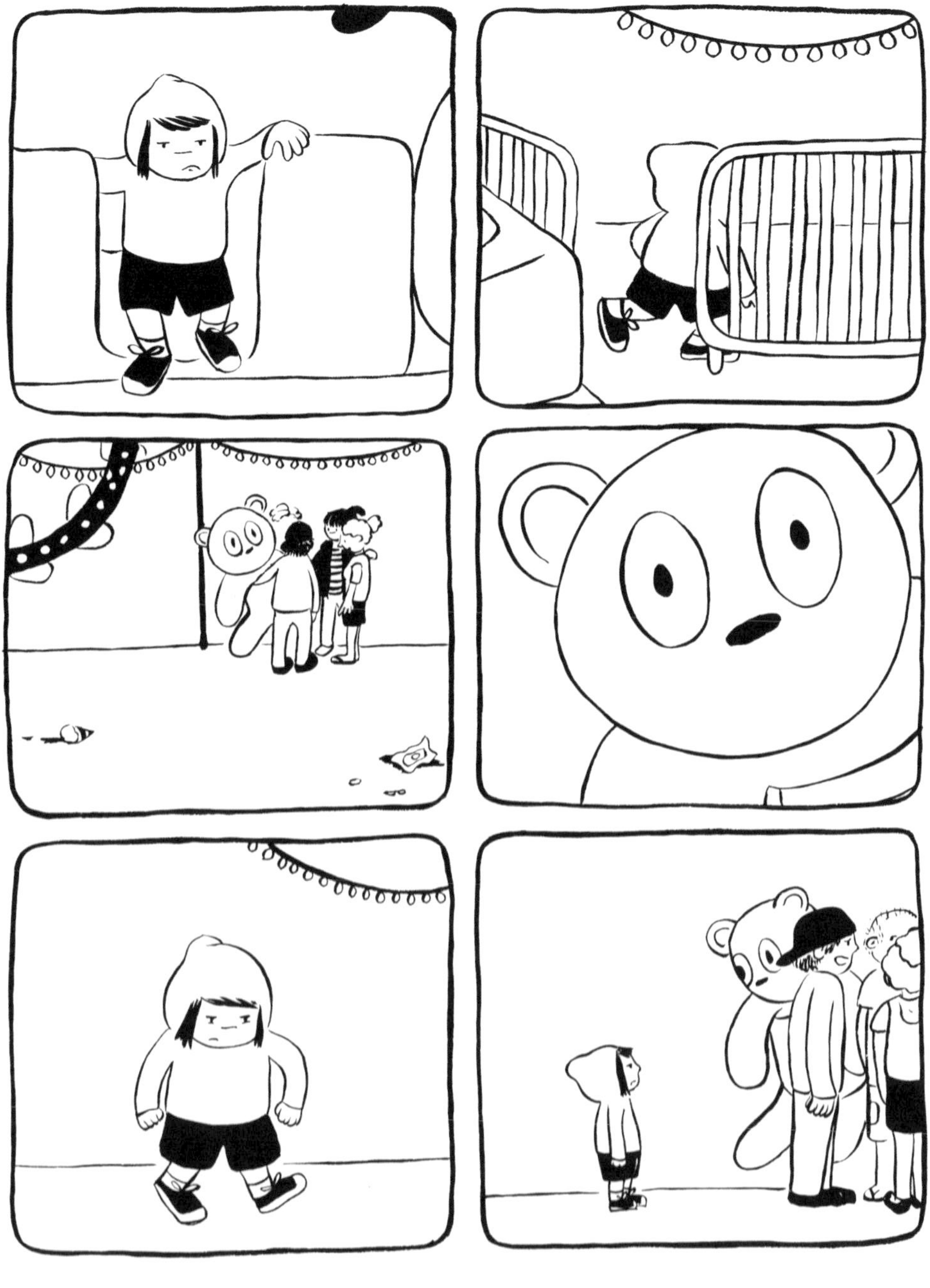

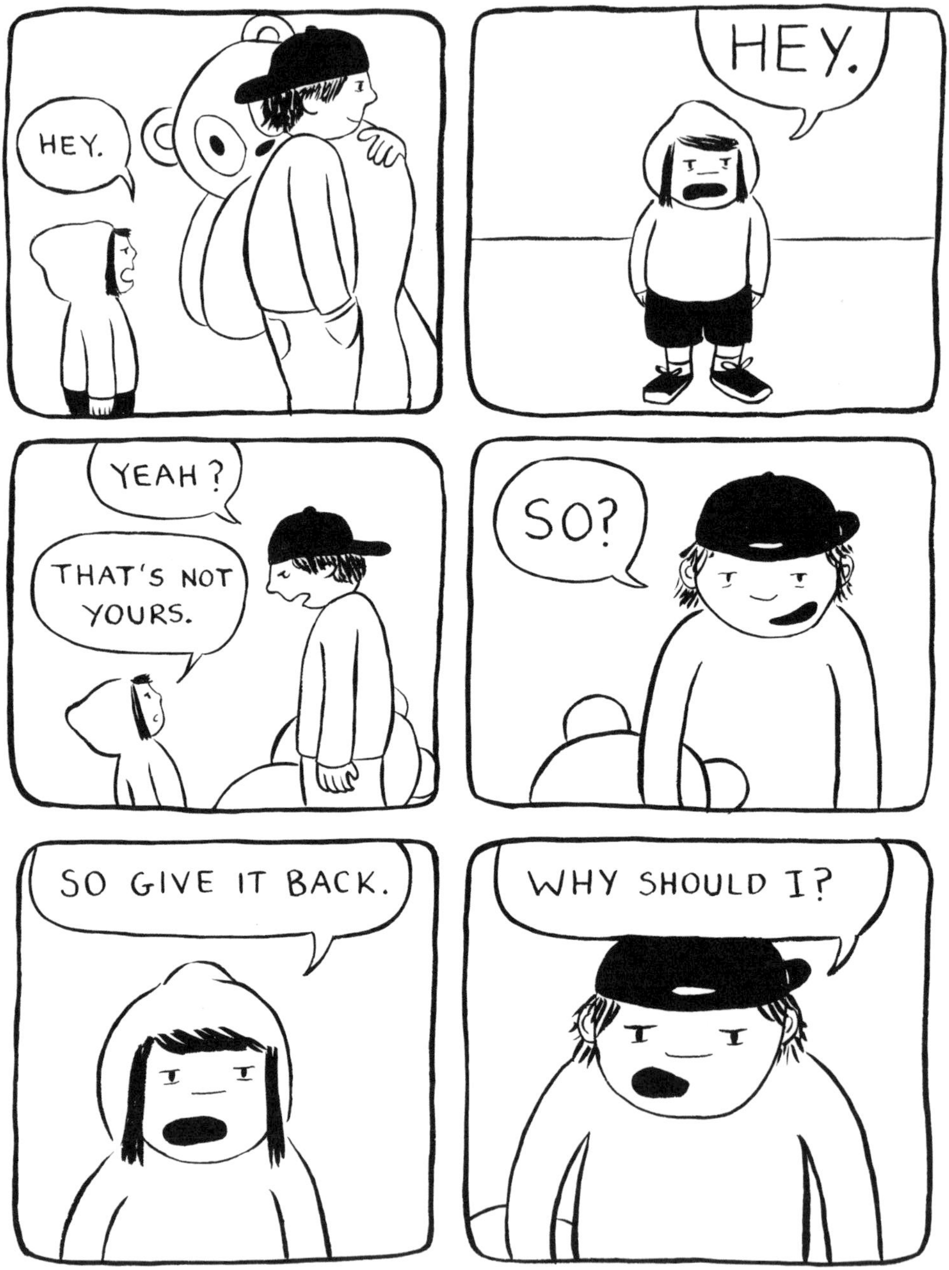
HEY.
HEY.
YEAH?
THAT'S NOT YOURS.
SO?
SO GIVE IT BACK.
WHY SHOULD I?

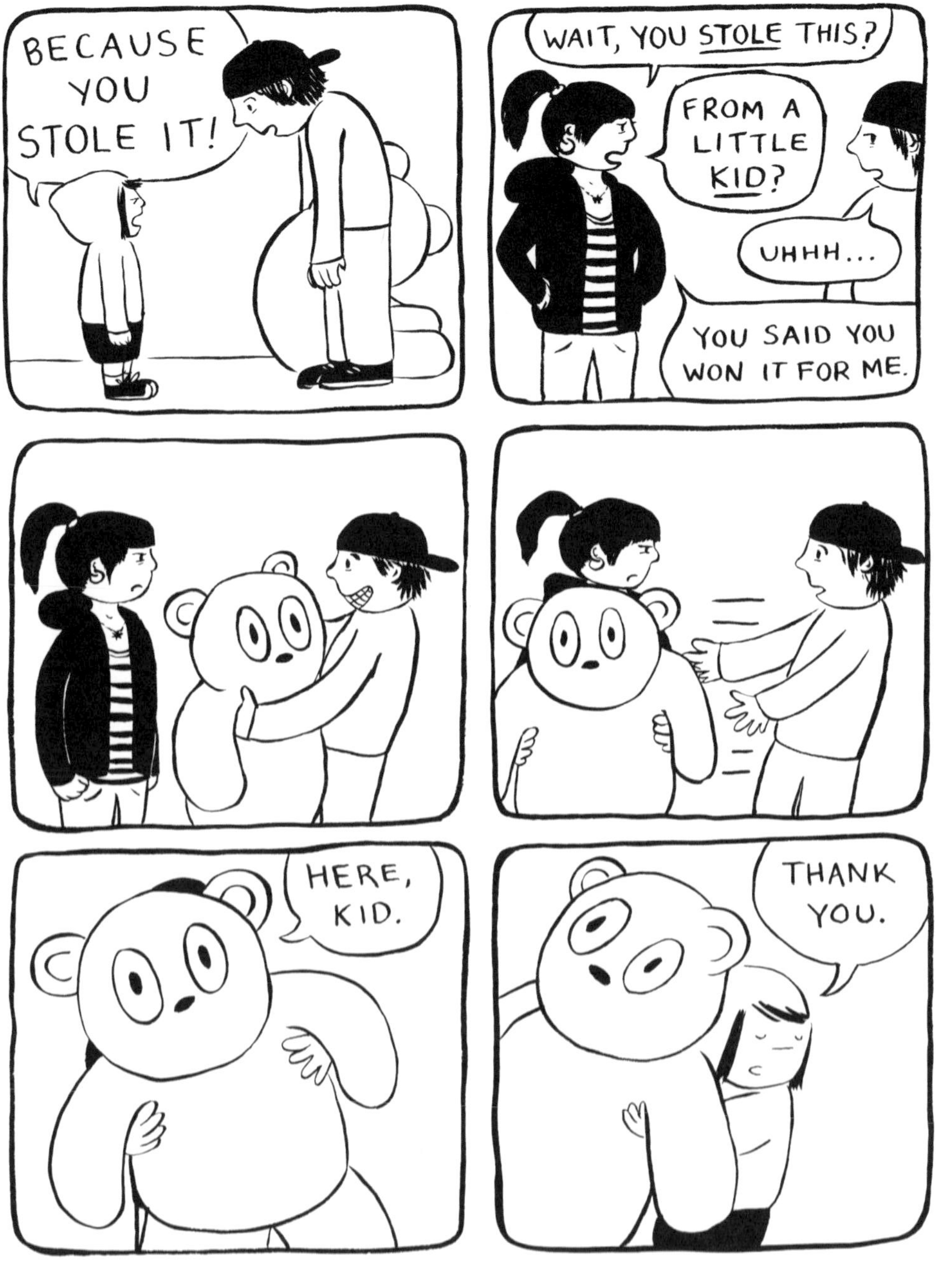
BECAUSE YOU STOLE IT!
WAIT, YOU STOLE THIS?
FROM A LITTLE KID?
UHHH...
YOU SAID YOU WON IT FOR ME.
HERE, KID.
THANK YOU.

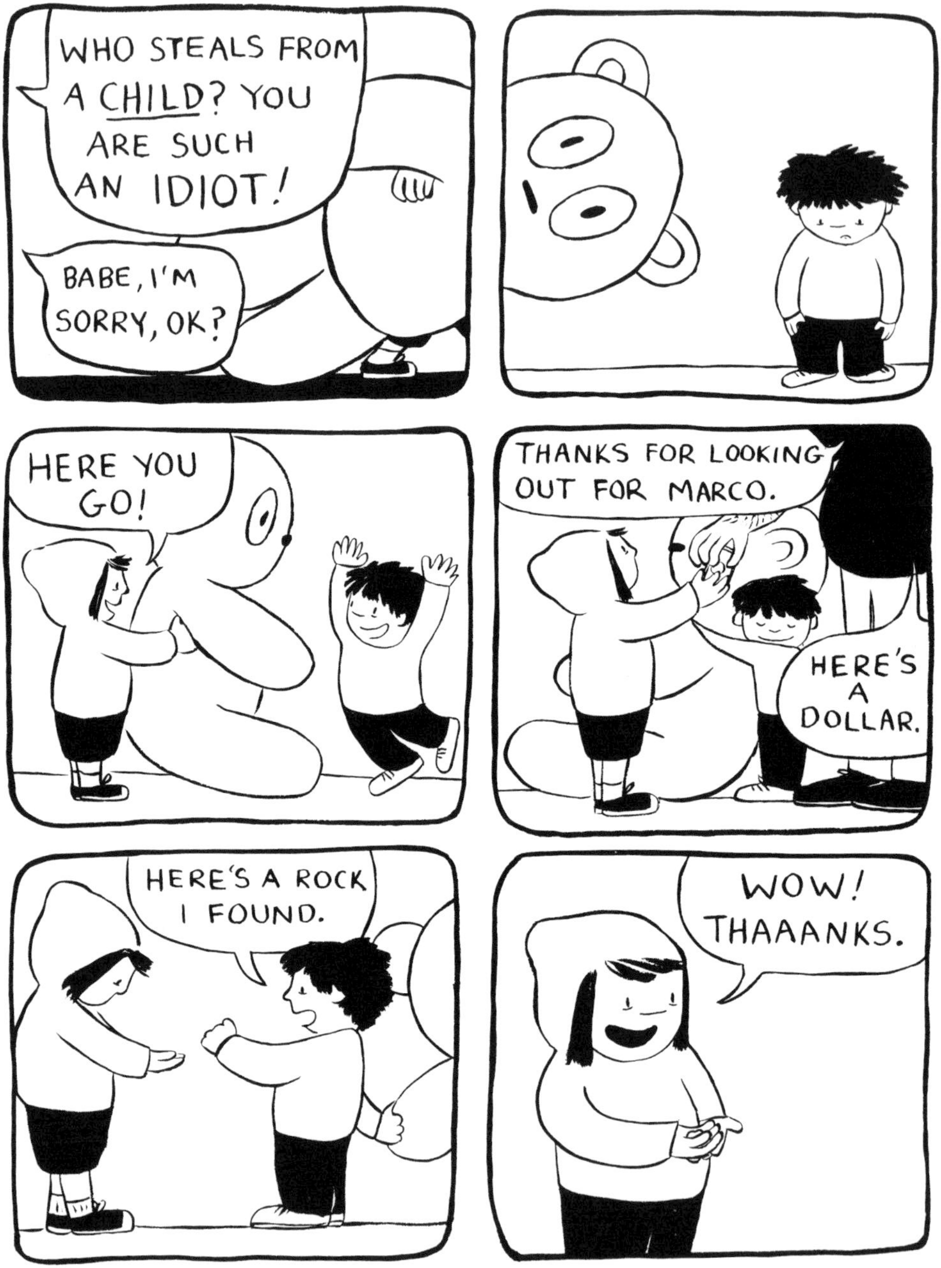
WHO STEALS FROM A CHILD? YOU ARE SUCH AN IDIOT!
BABE, I'M SORRY, OK?
HERE YOU GO!
THANKS FOR LOOKING OUT FOR MARCO.
HERE'S A DOLLAR.
HERE'S A ROCK I FOUND.
WOW! THAAANKS.

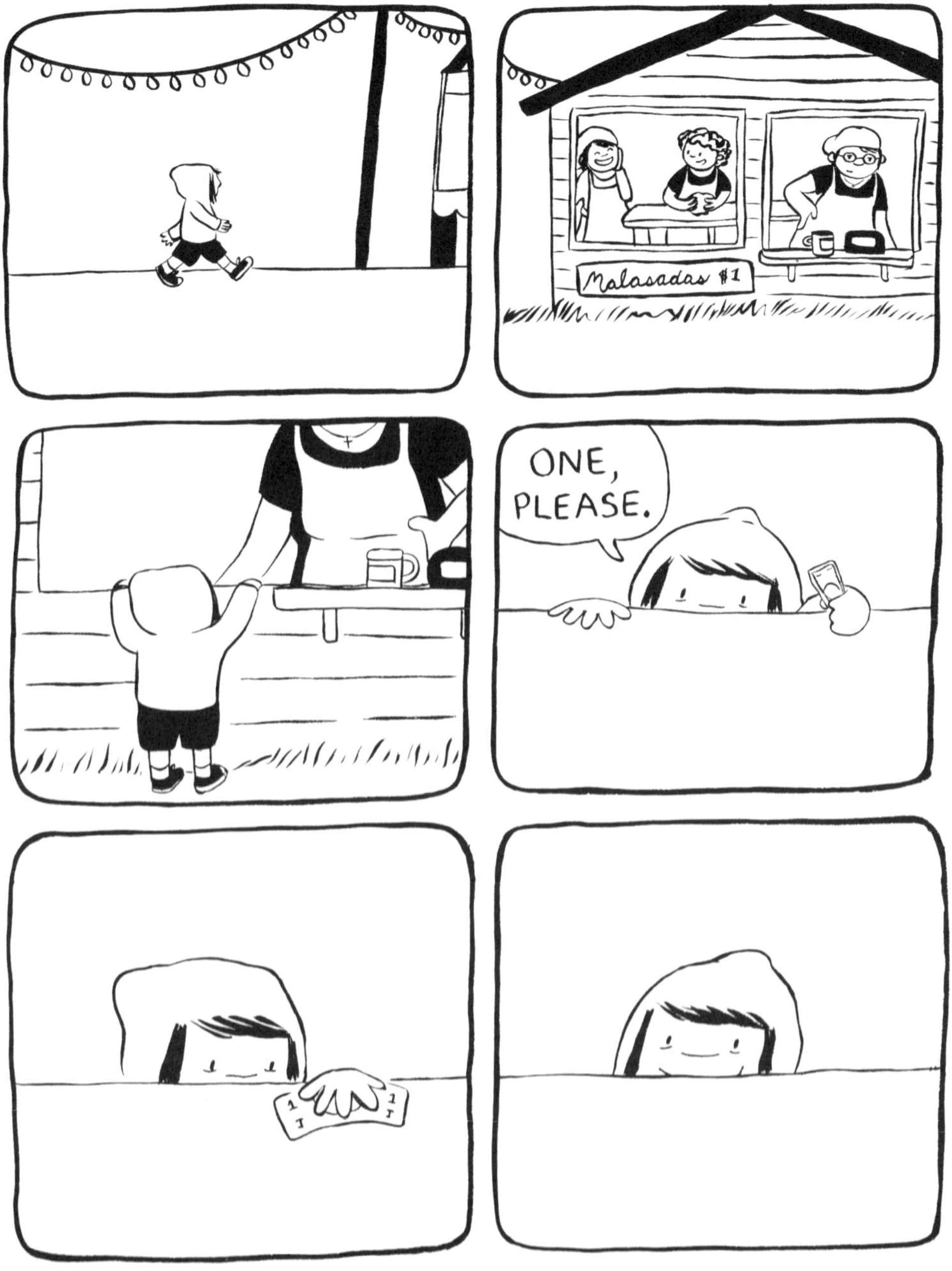
Malasadas #1
ONE, PLEASE.

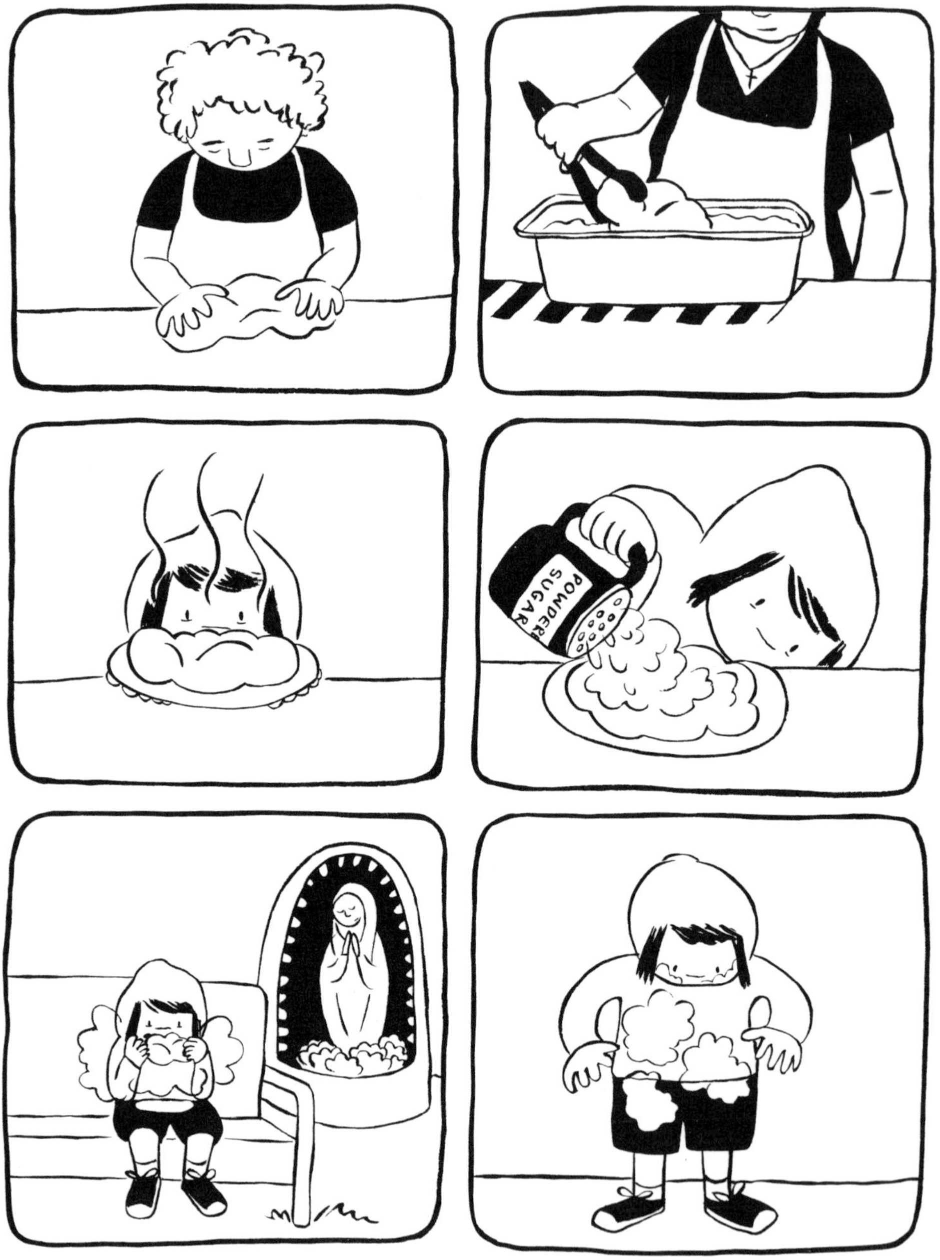
POWDER SUGAR

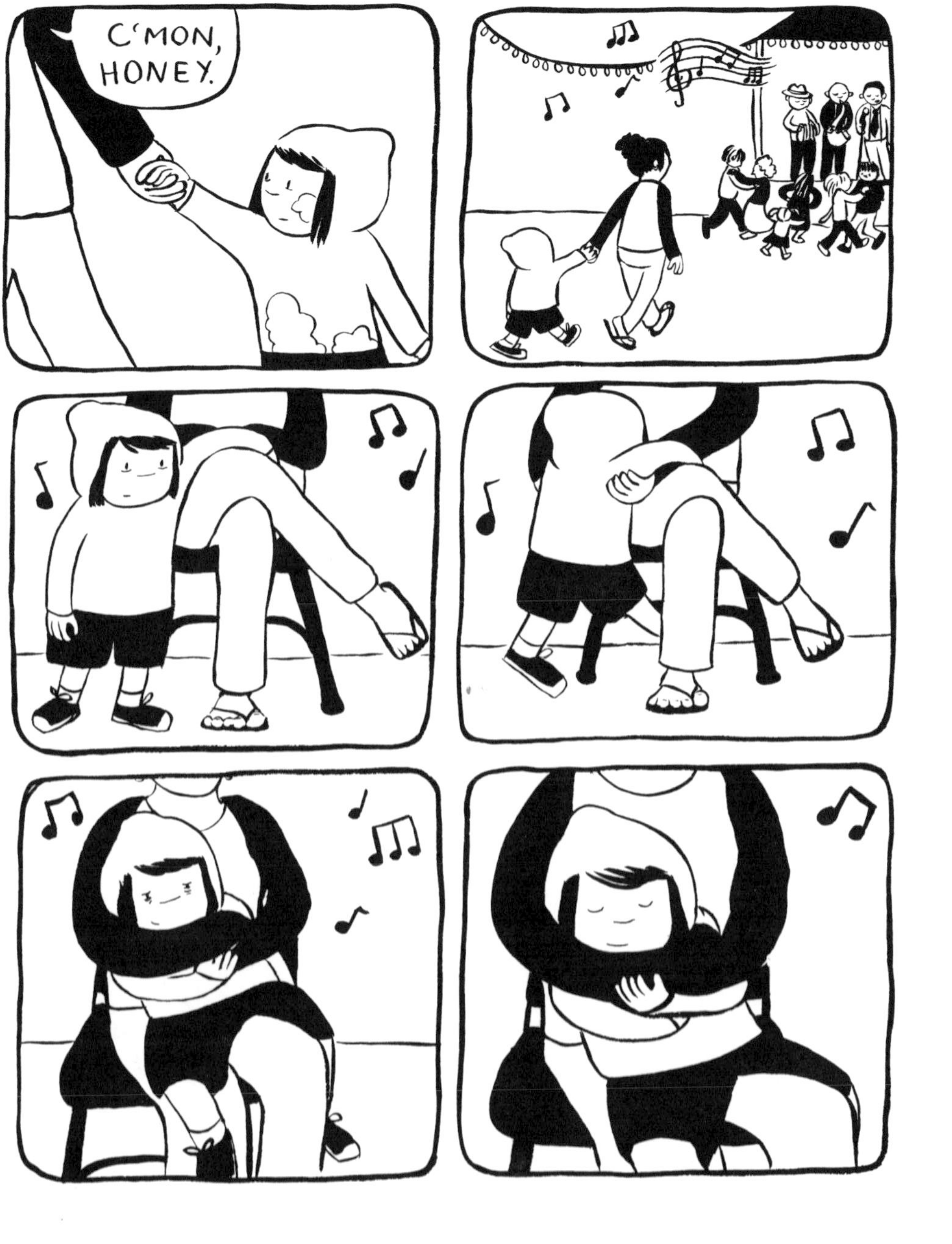
C'MON, HONEY.

BIRTHDAY

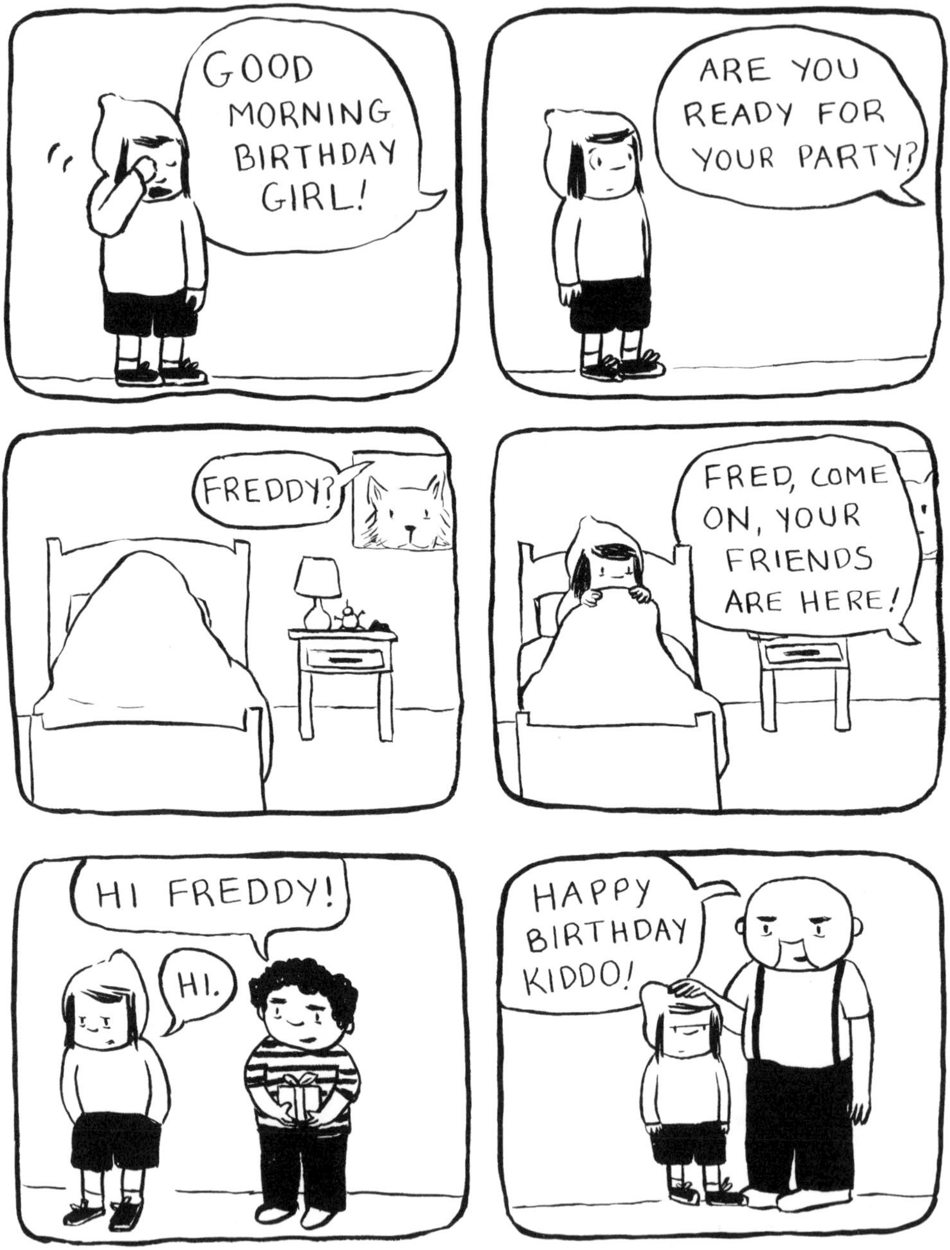
GOOD MORNING BIRTHDAY GIRL!
ARE YOU READY FOR YOUR PARTY?
FREDDY?
FRED, COME ON, YOUR FRIENDS ARE HERE!
HI FREDDY!
HI.
HAPPY BIRTHDAY KIDDO!

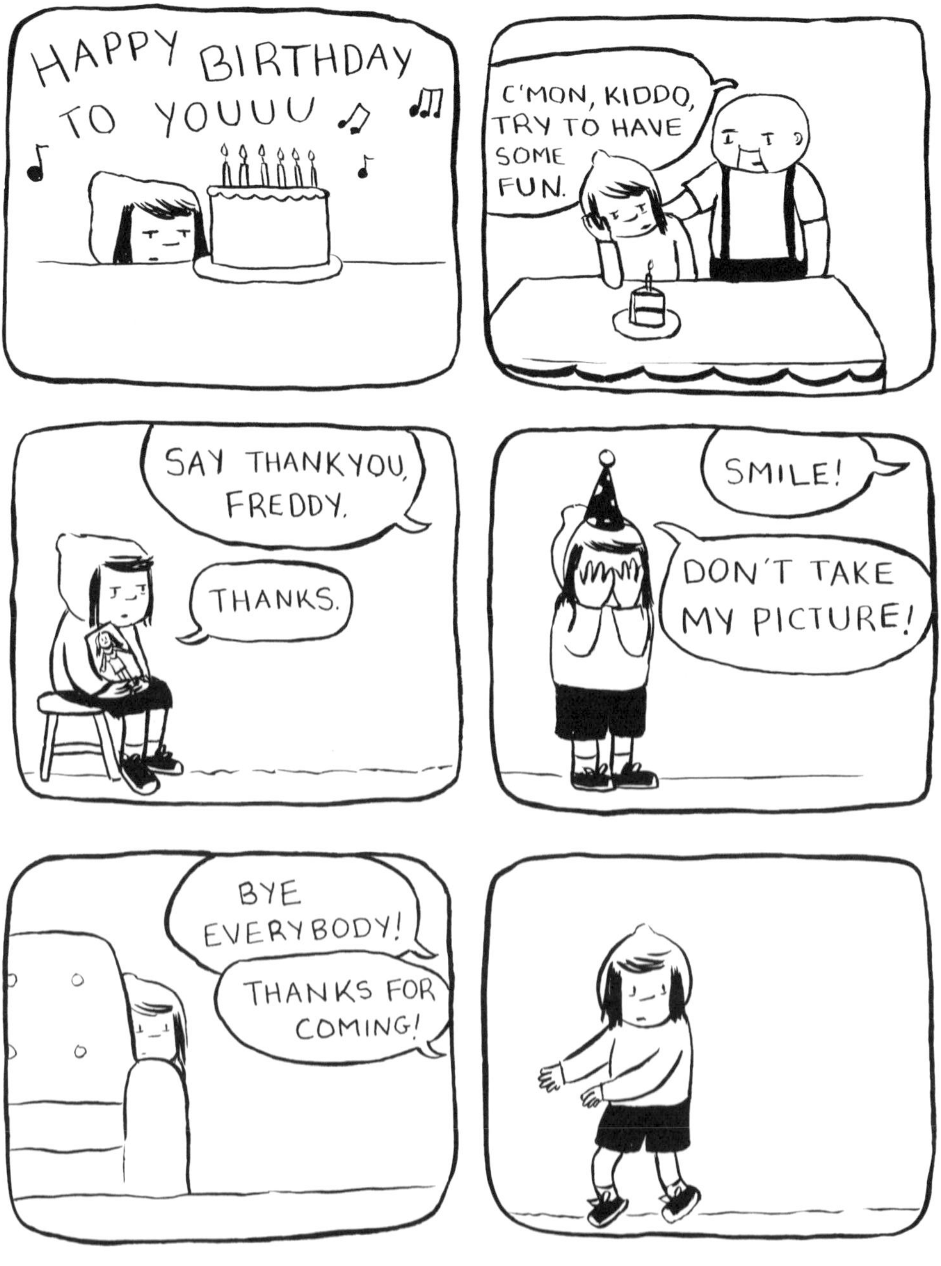
HAPPY BIRTHDAY TO YOUUU
C'MON, KIDDO, TRY TO HAVE SOME FUN.
SAY THANKYOU, FREDDY.
THANKS.
SMILE!
DON'T TAKE MY PICTURE!
BYE EVERYBODY!
THANKS FOR COMING!

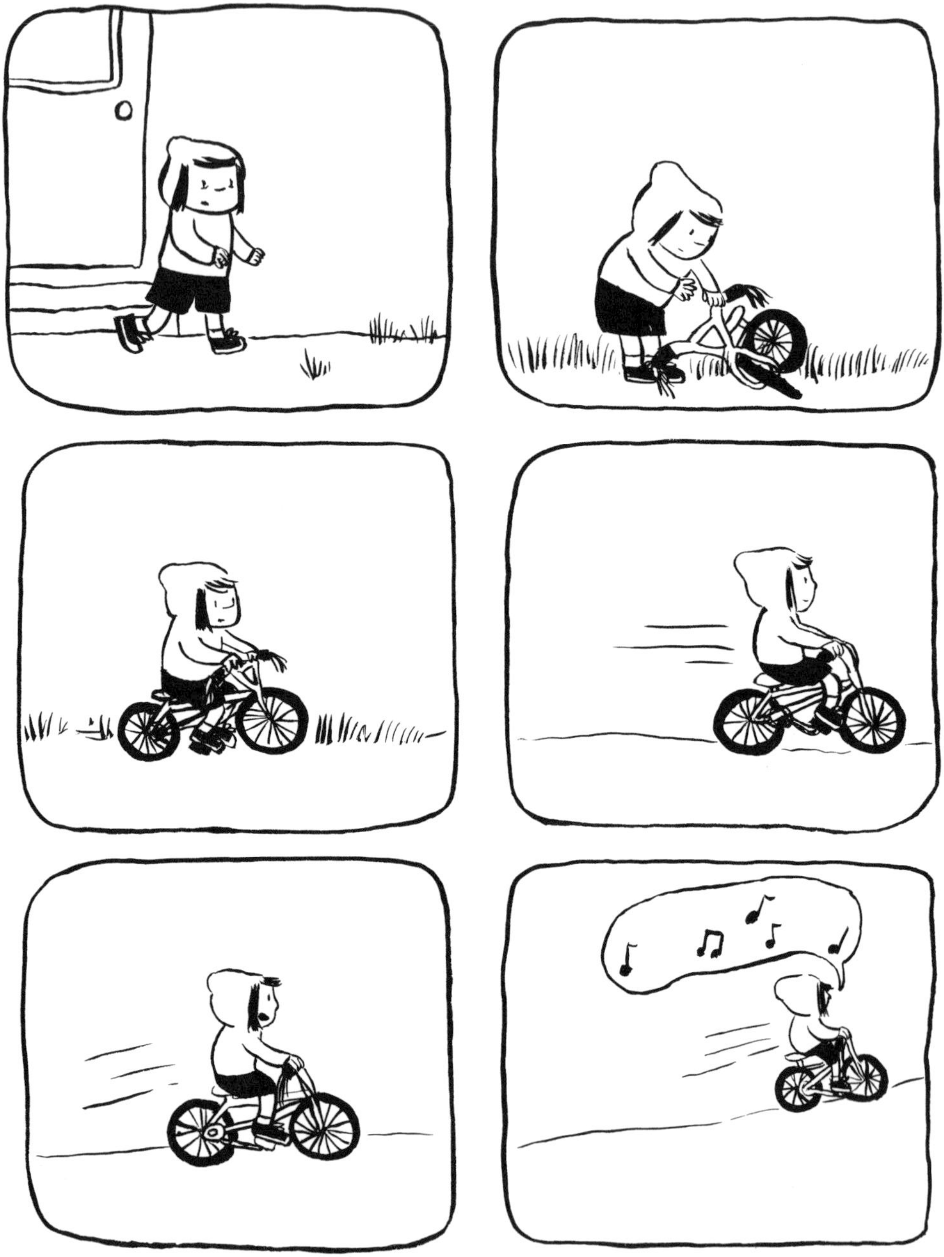

DISHES

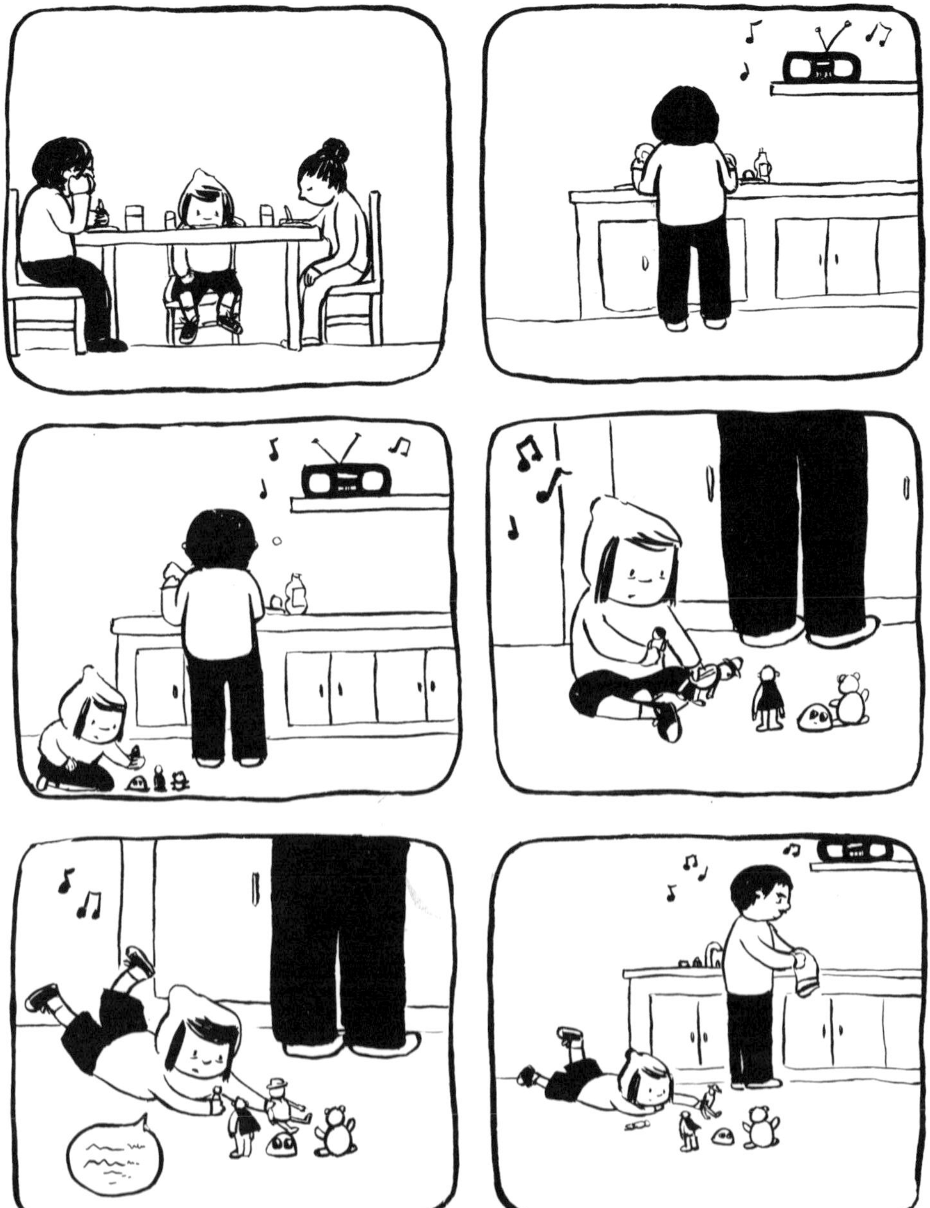

AWAKE

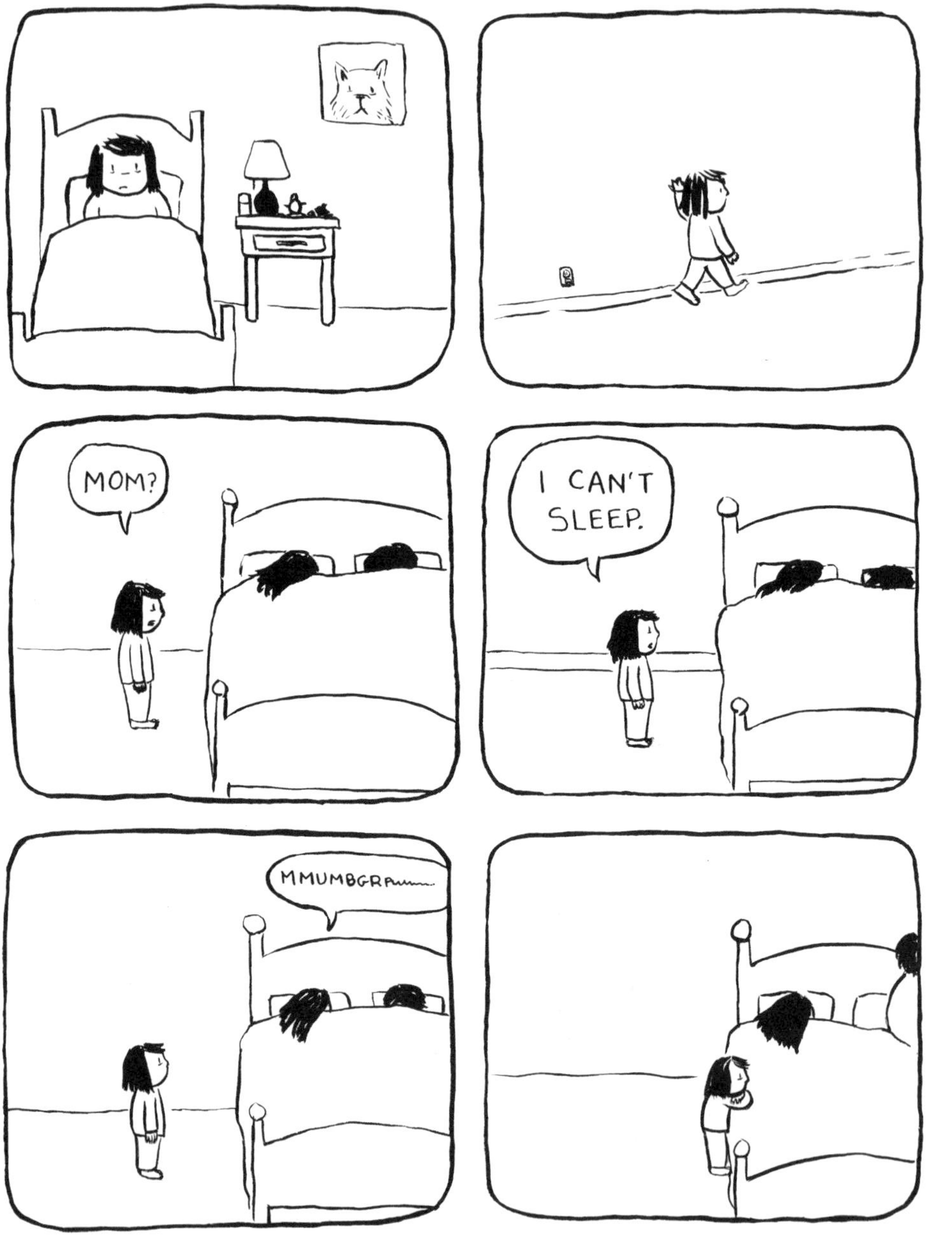
MOM?
I CAN'T SLEEP.
MMUMBGRA

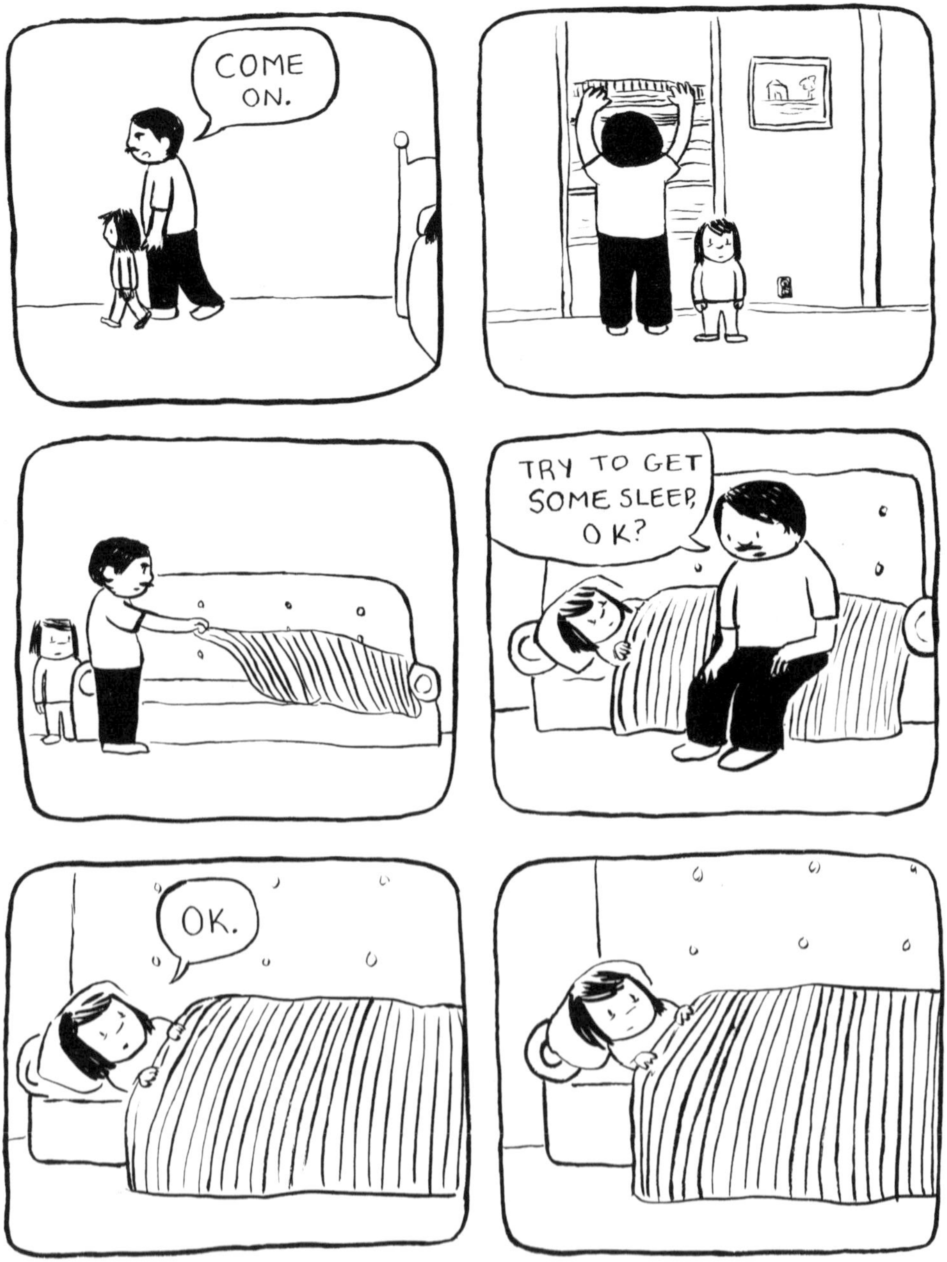
COME ON.
TRY TO GET SOME SLEEP, OK?
OK.

WIFFLE BALL

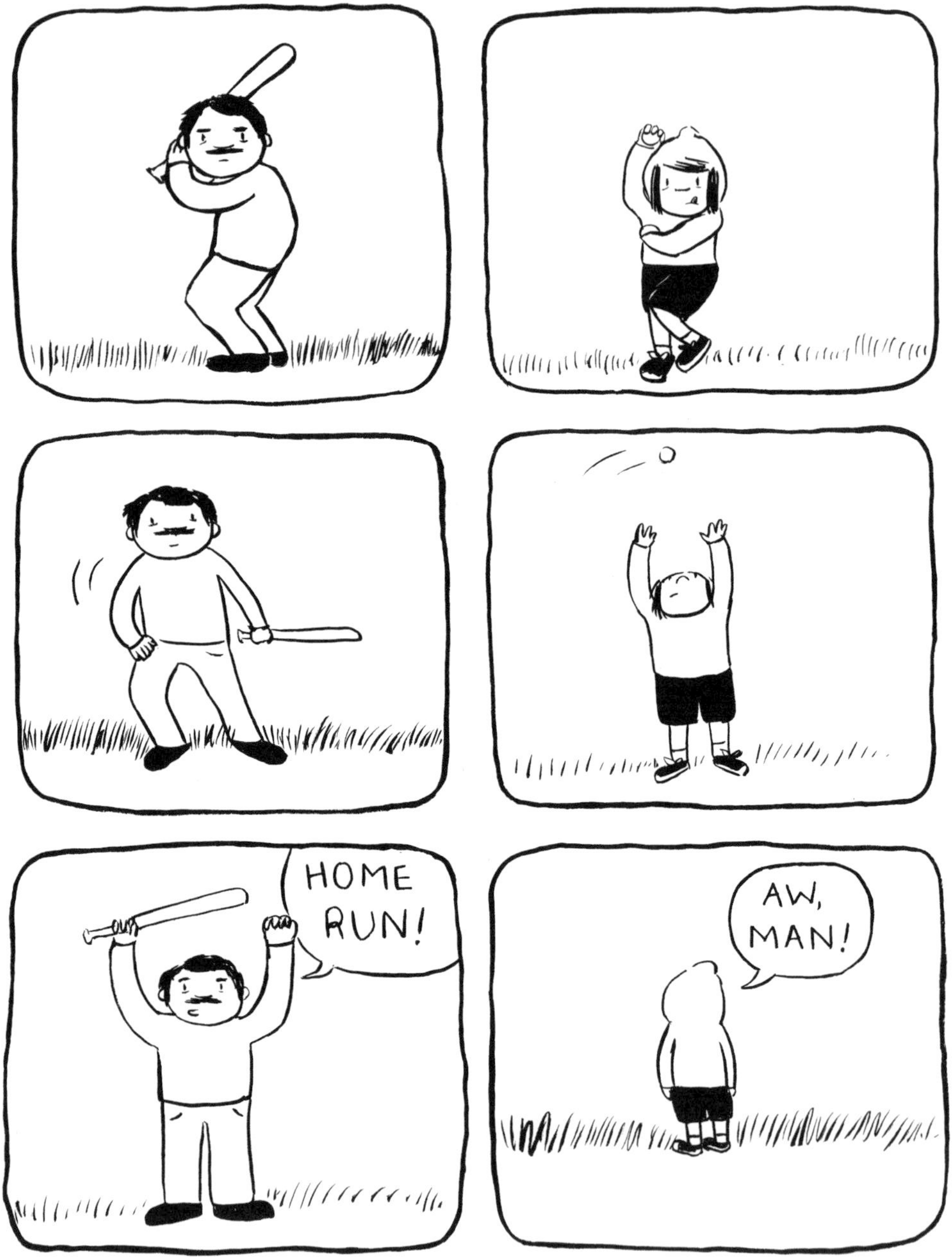
HOME RUN!
AW, MAN!

DAD'S HOUSE

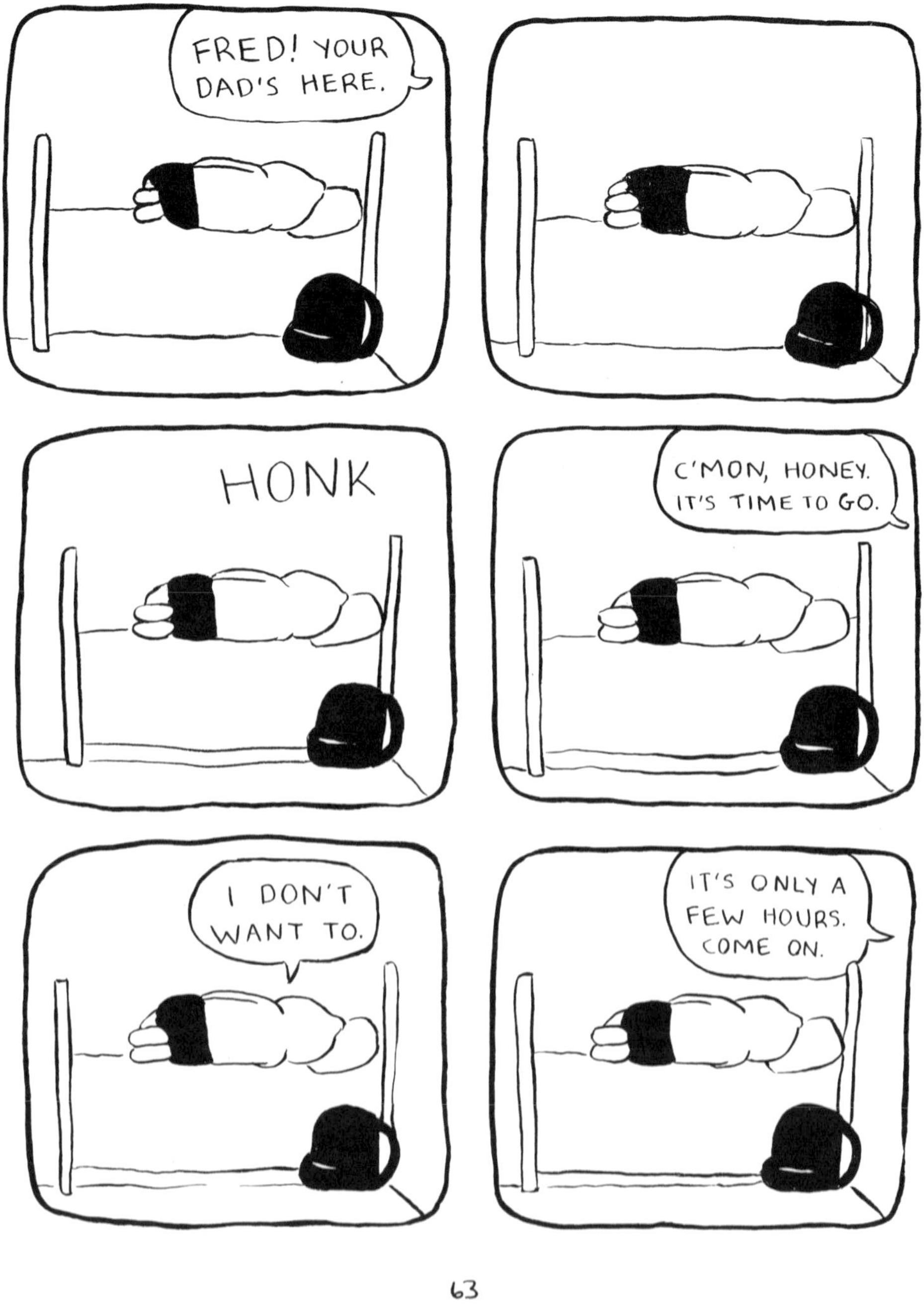
FRED! YOUR DAD'S HERE.
HONK
C'MON, HONEY. IT'S TIME TO GO.
I DON'T WANT TO.
IT'S ONLY A FEW HOURS. COME ON.

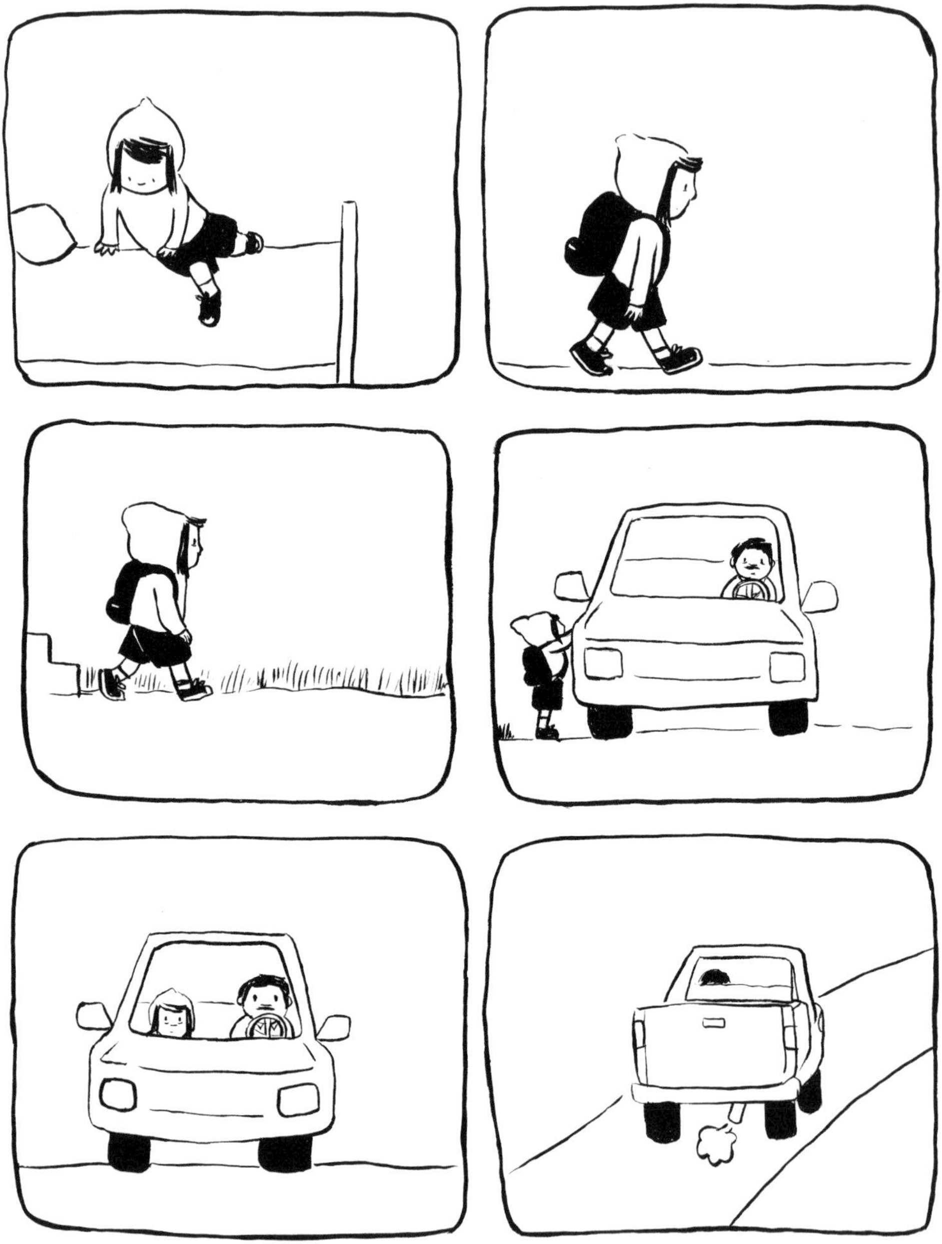

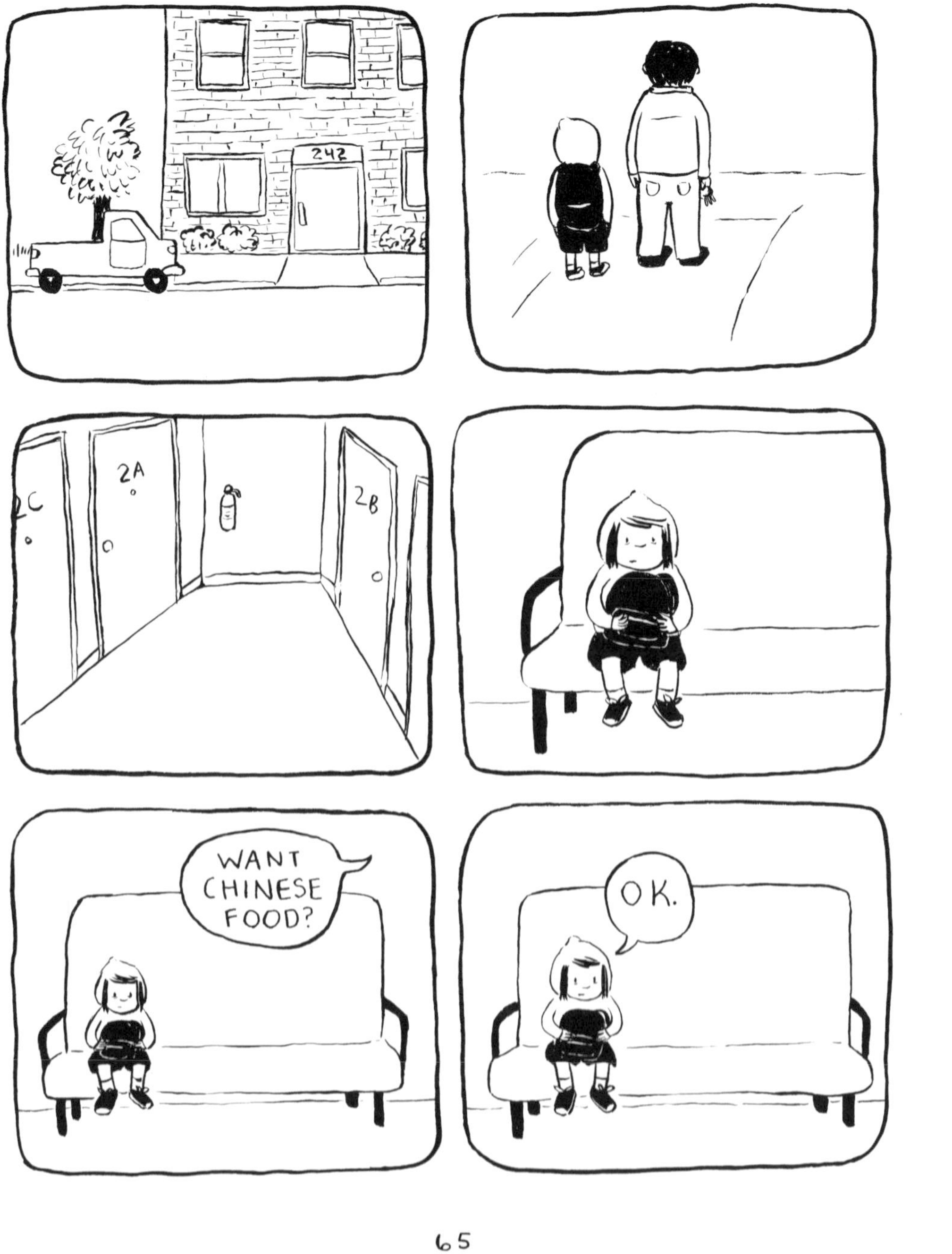
242
2A
2C
2B
WANT CHINESE FOOD?
OK.

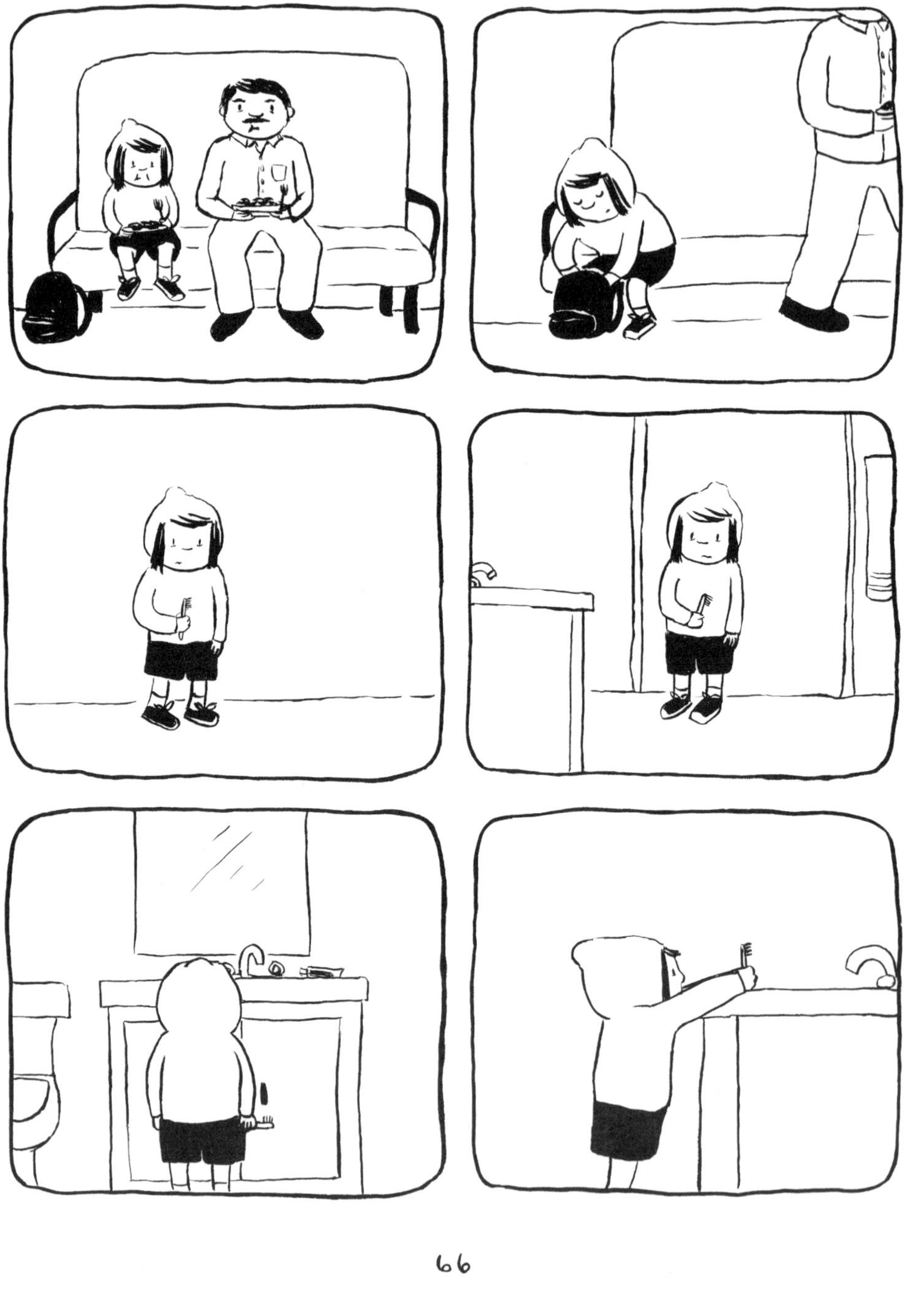

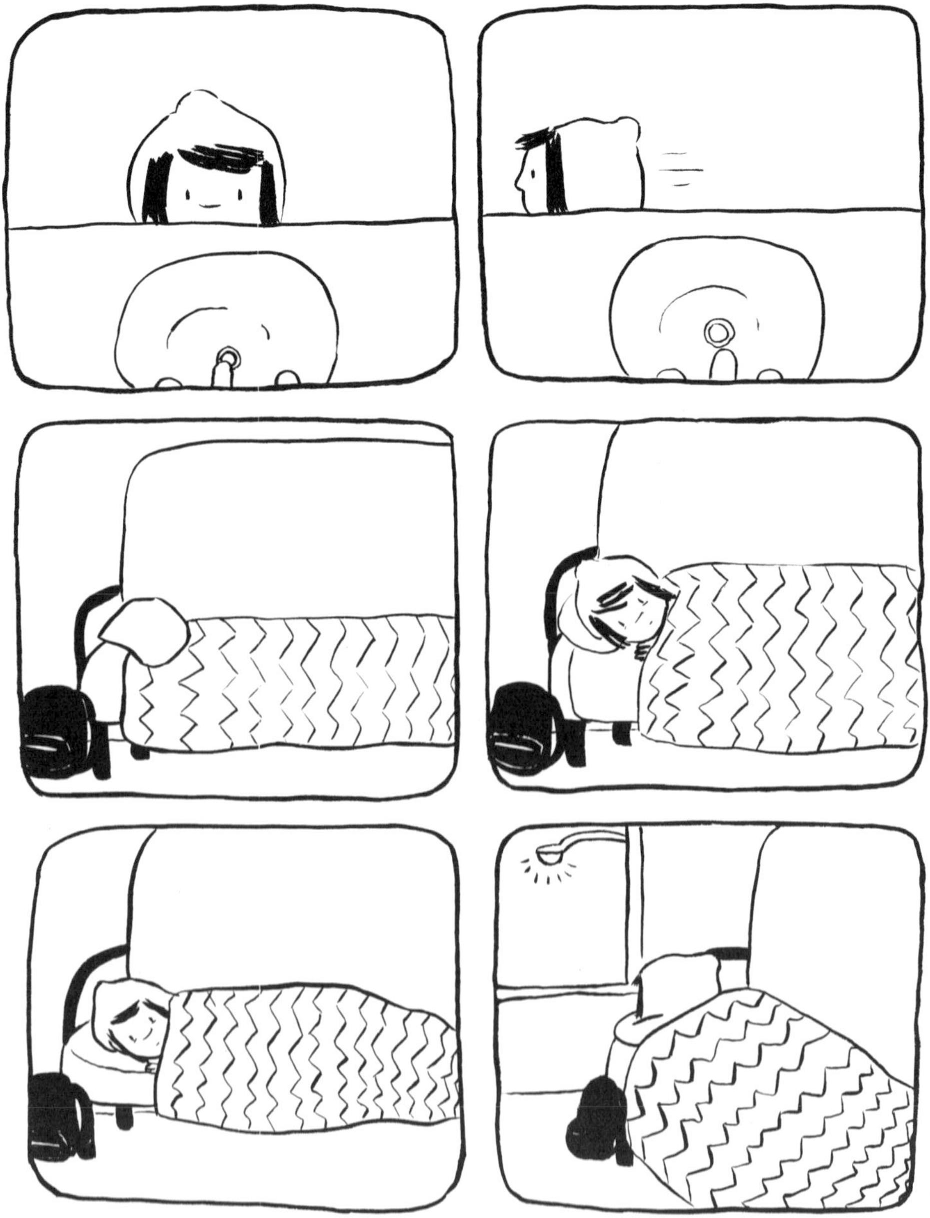

RECESS

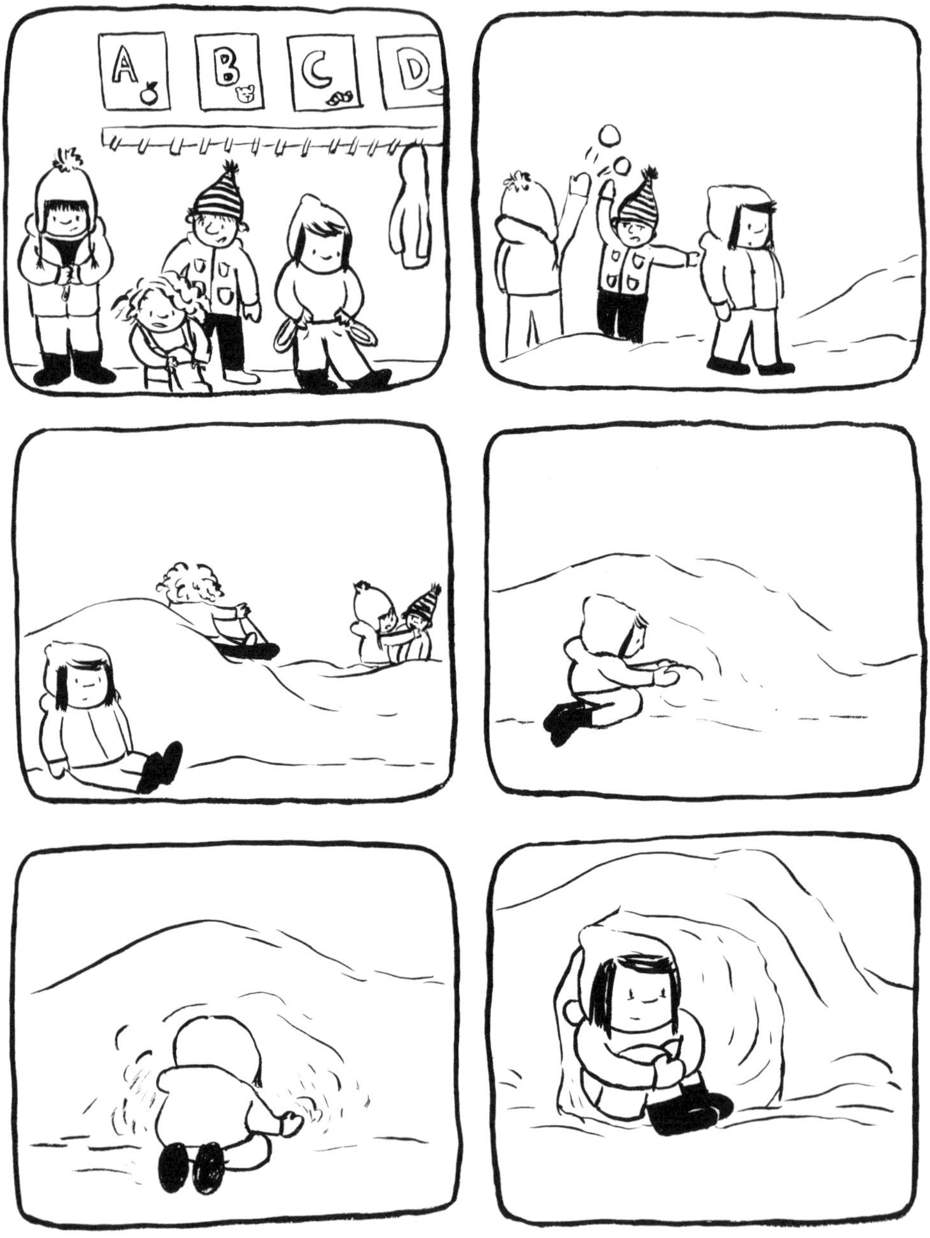
A
B
C
D

RUNAWAY

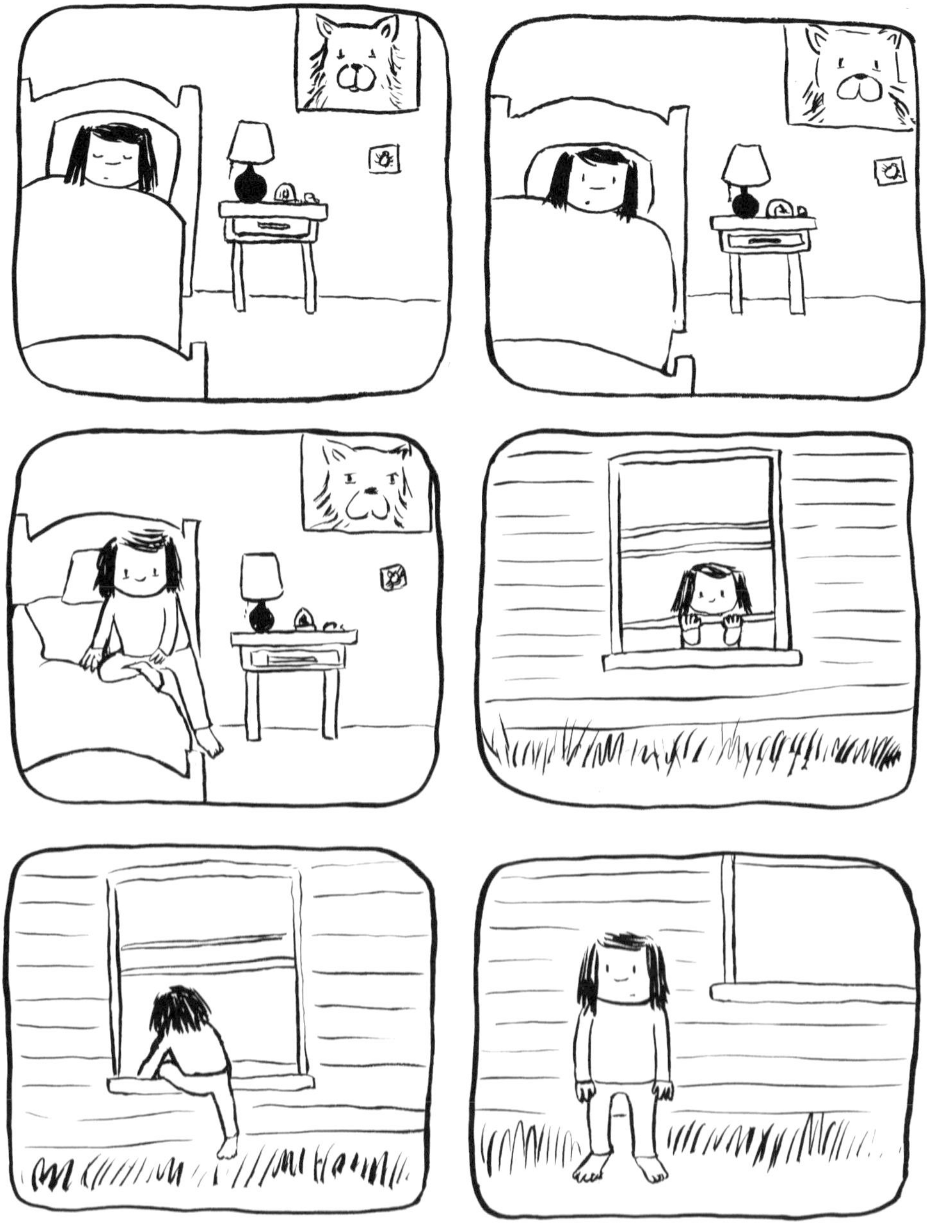

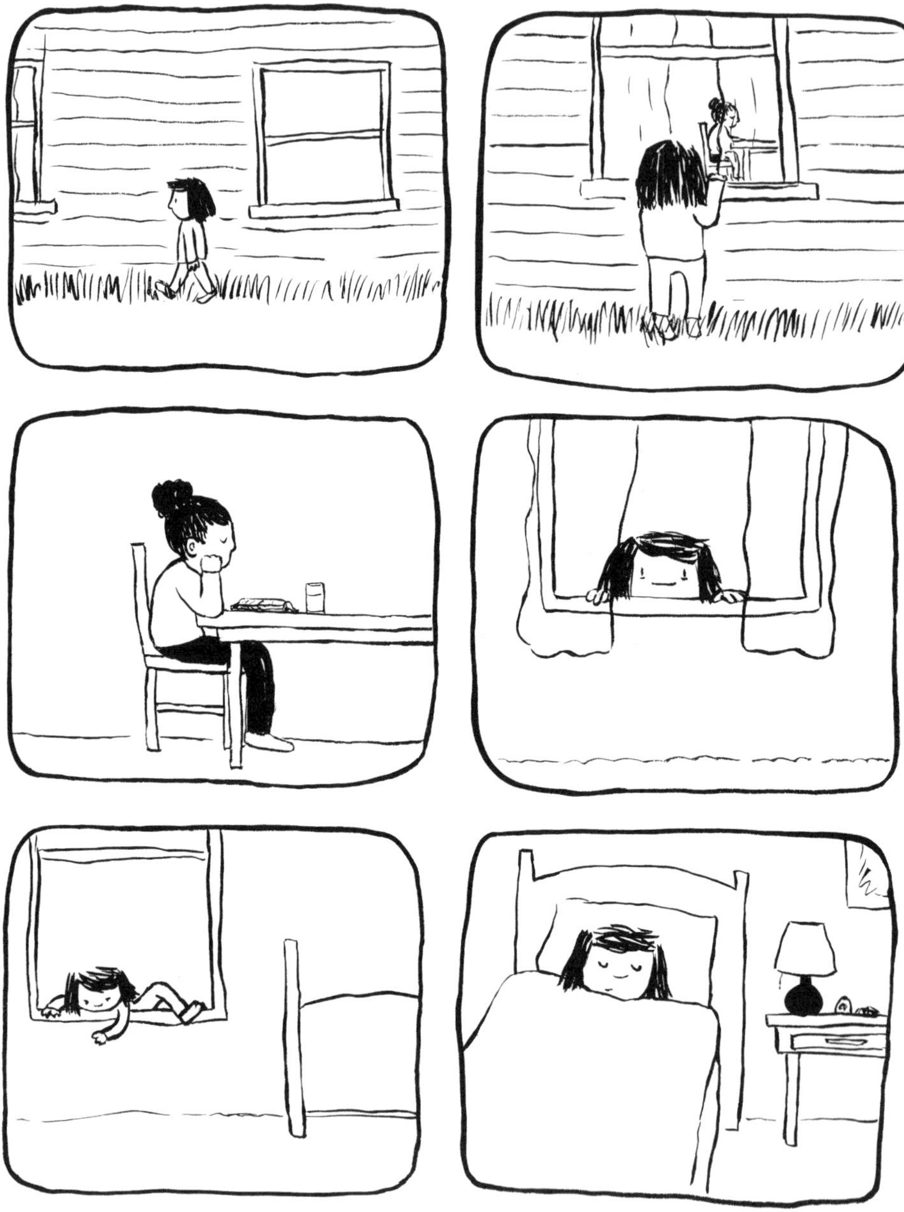

CHURCH

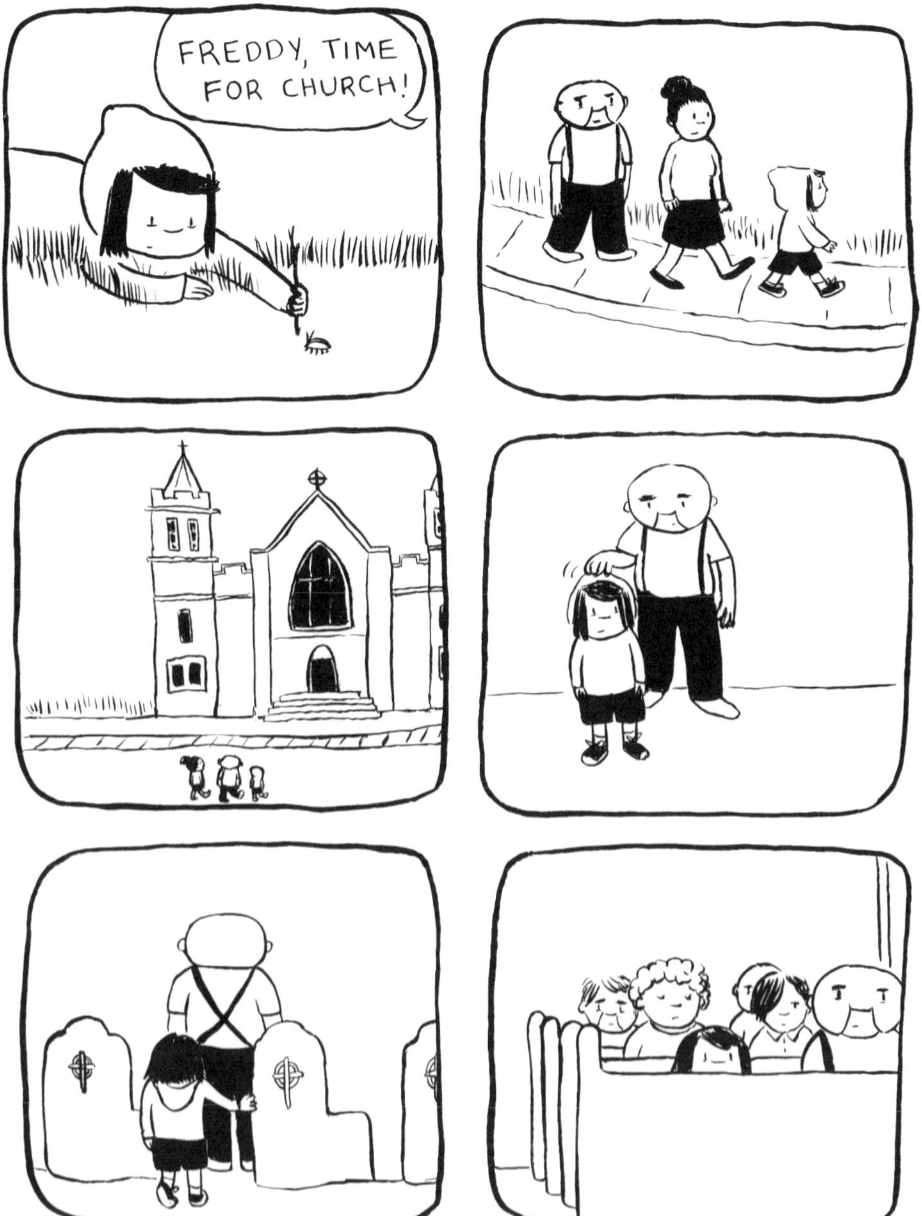
FREDDY, TIME FOR CHURCH!

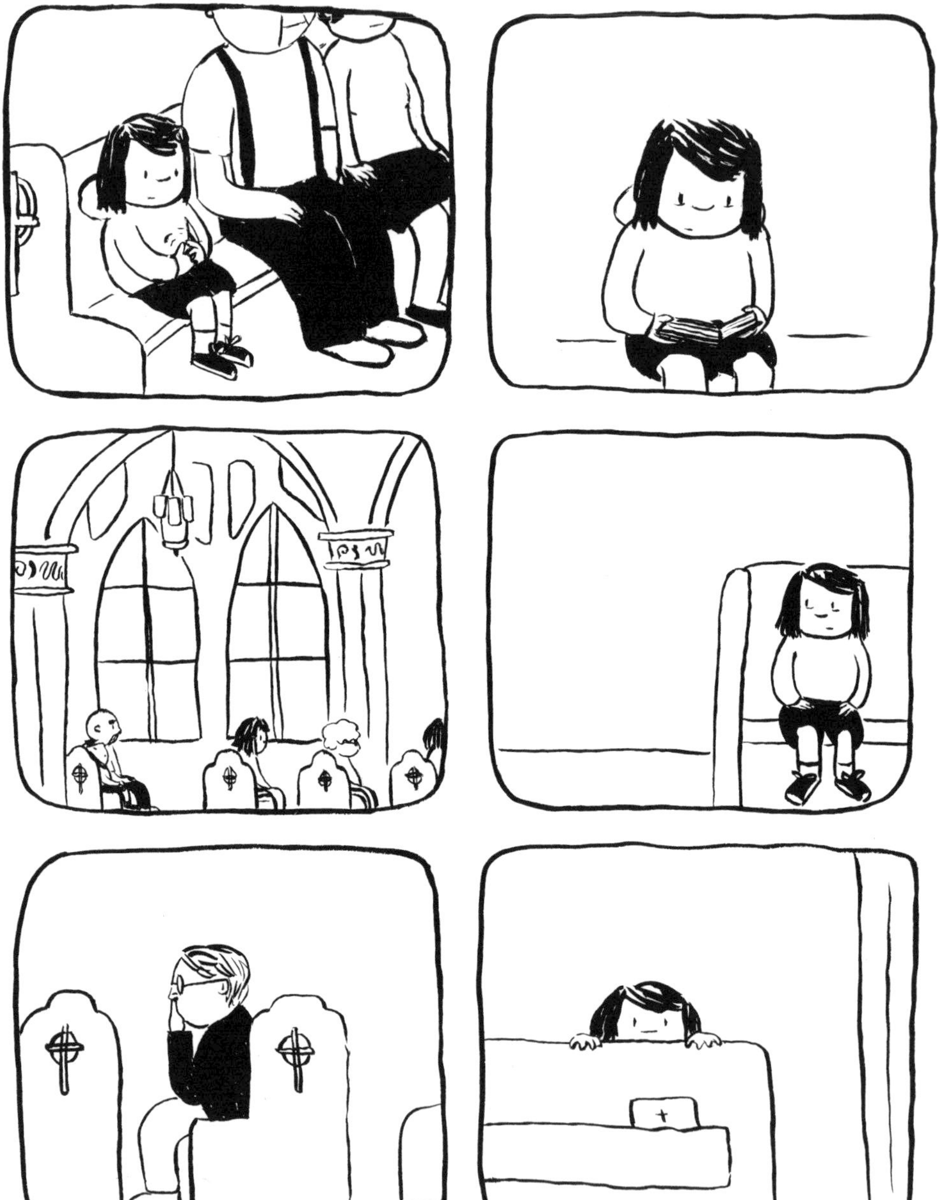

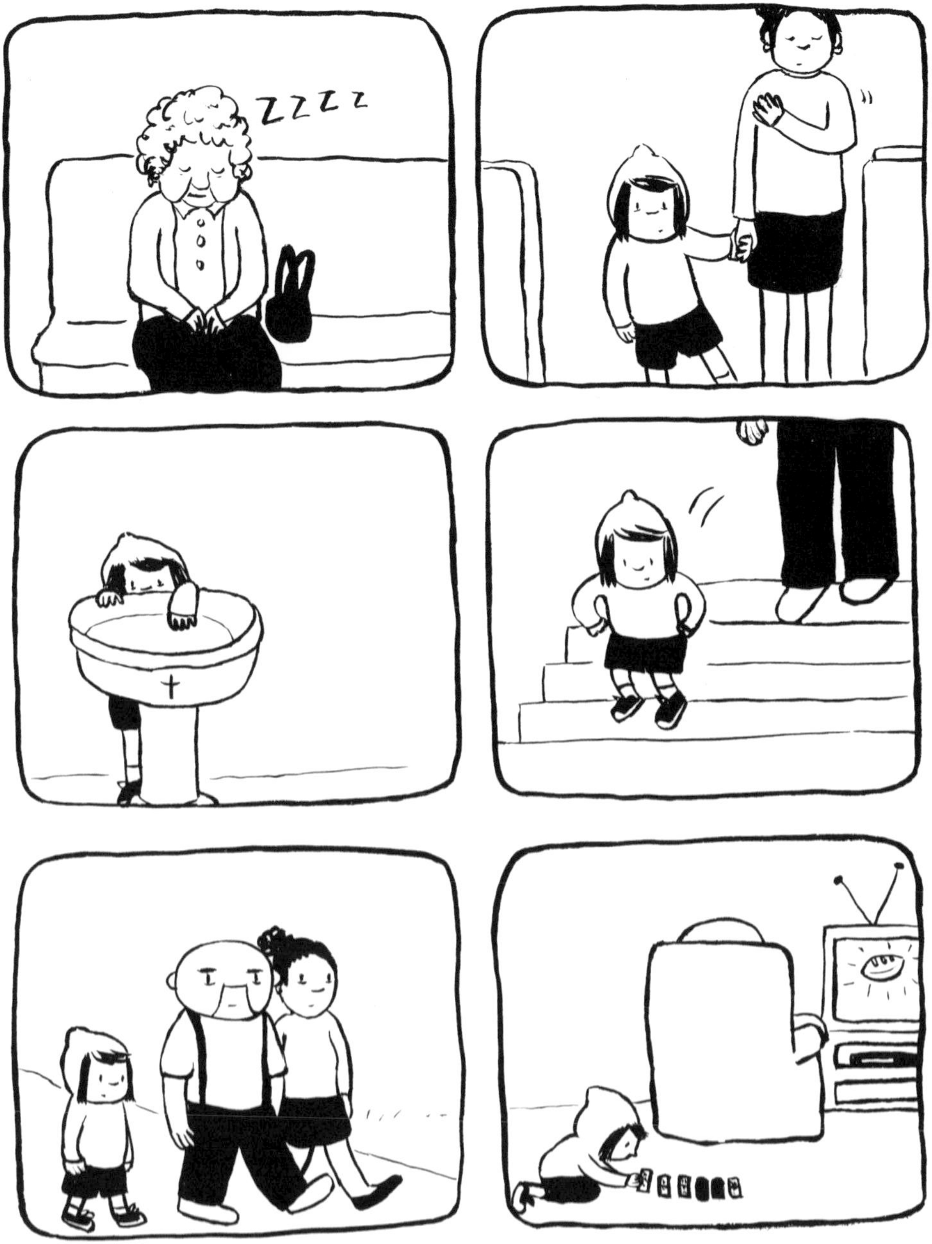
ZZZZ

PINBALL

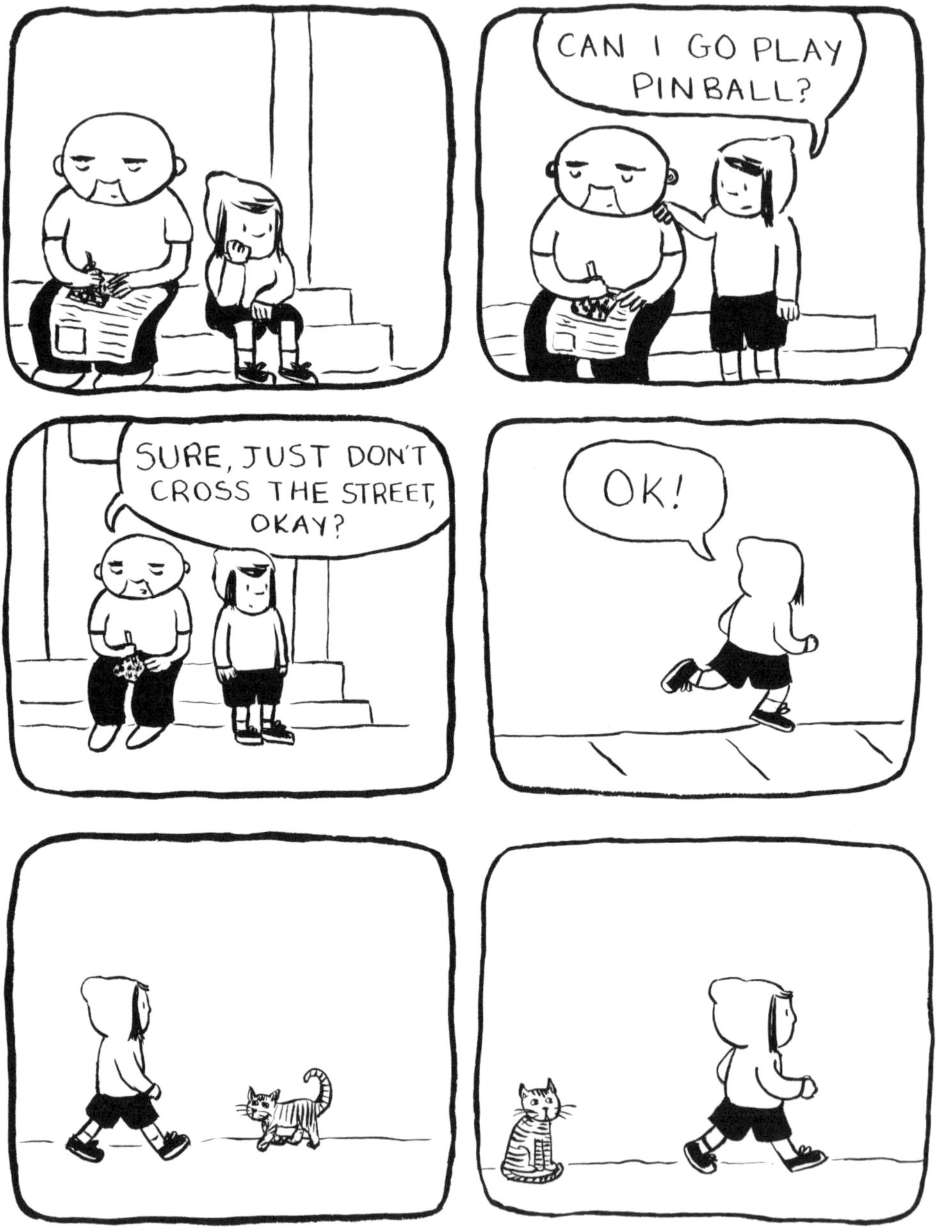
CAN I GO PLAY PINBALL?
SURE, JUST DON'T CROSS THE STREET, OKAY?
OK!

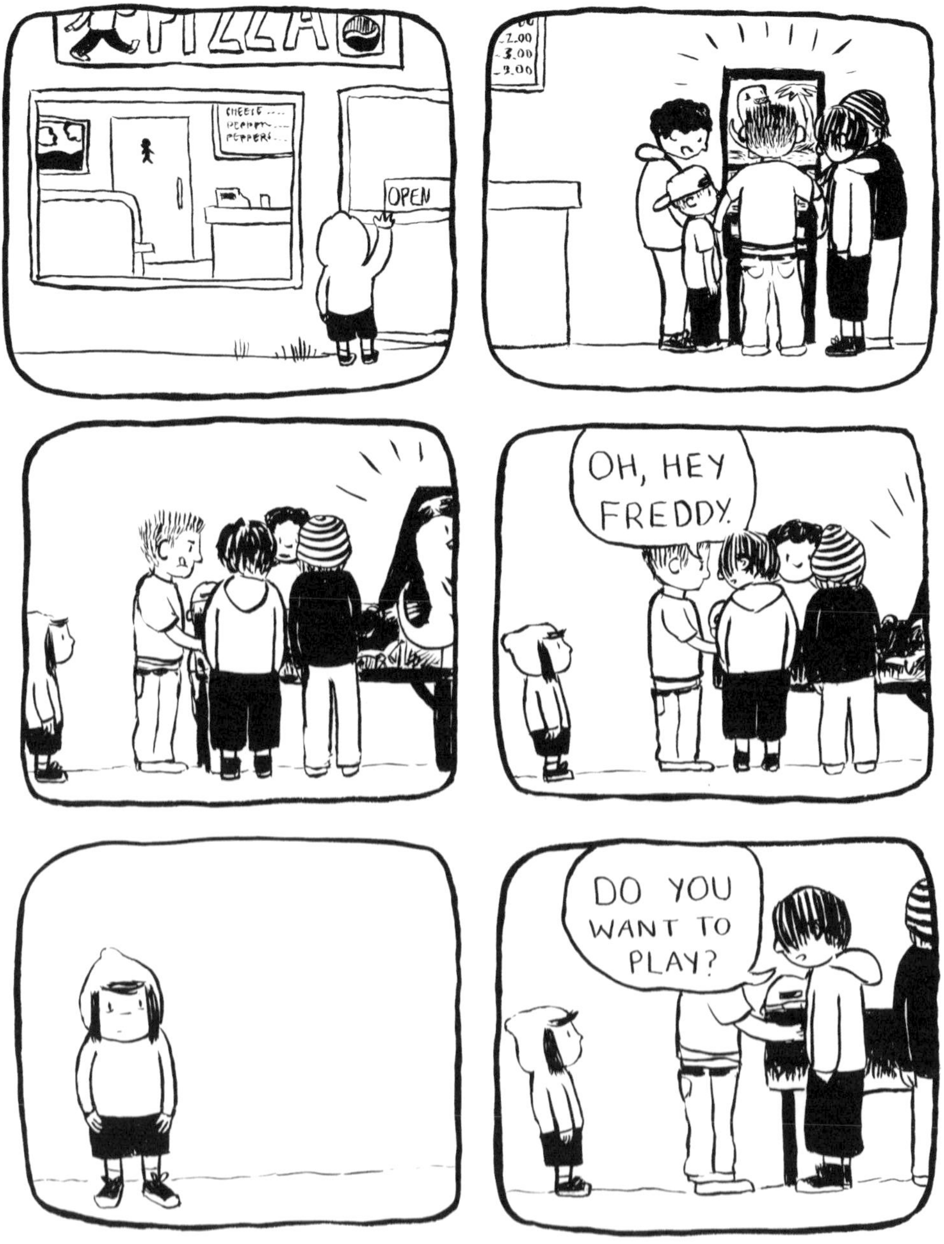
PIZZA
OPEN
OH, HEY FREDDY.
DO YOU WANT TO PLAY?

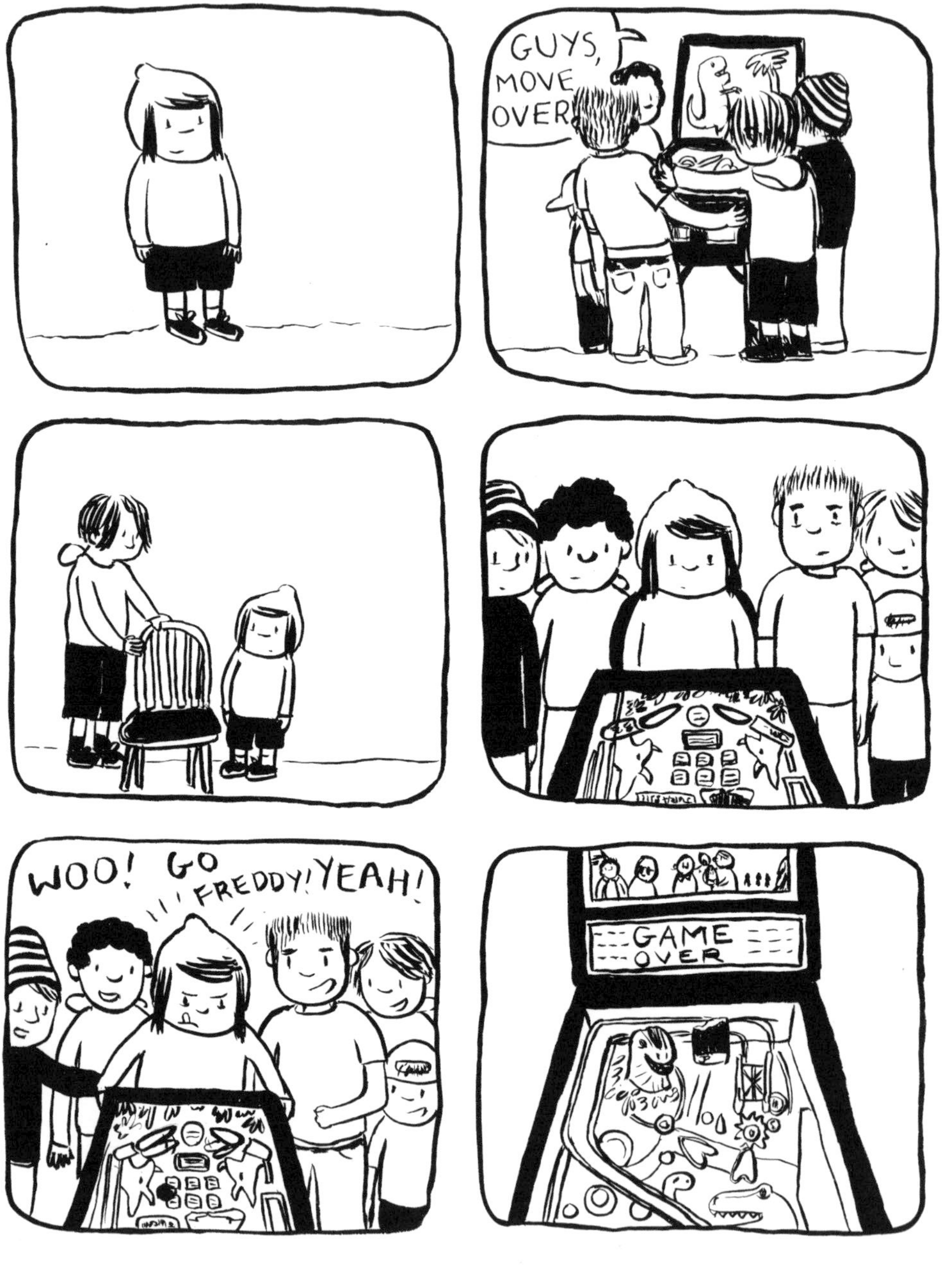

GUYS, MOVE OVER!
WOO! GO FREDDY! YEAH!
GAME OVER

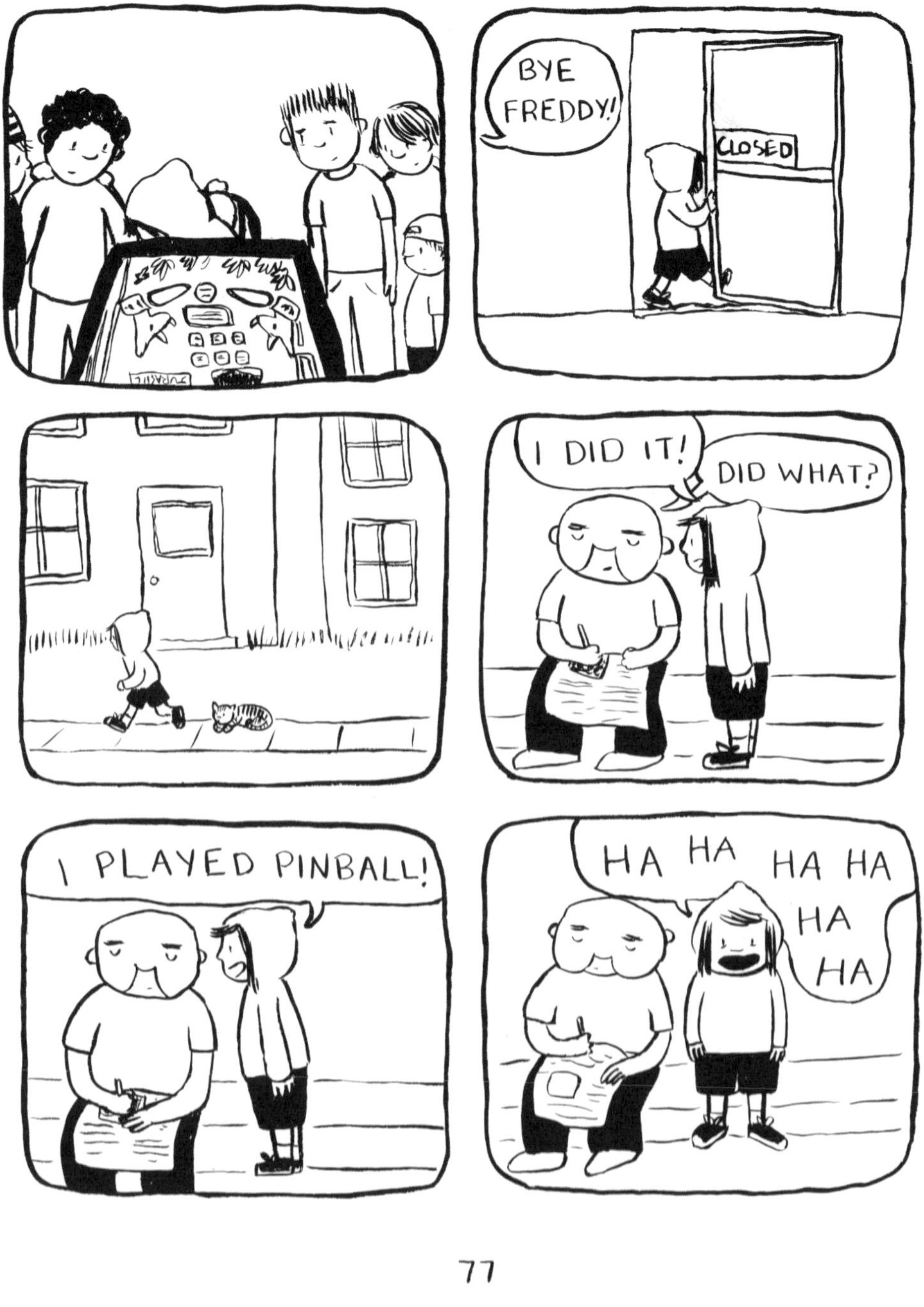
BYE FREDDY!
CLOSED
I DID IT!
DID WHAT?
I PLAYED PINBALL!
HA HA HA HA HA HA HA

JOE

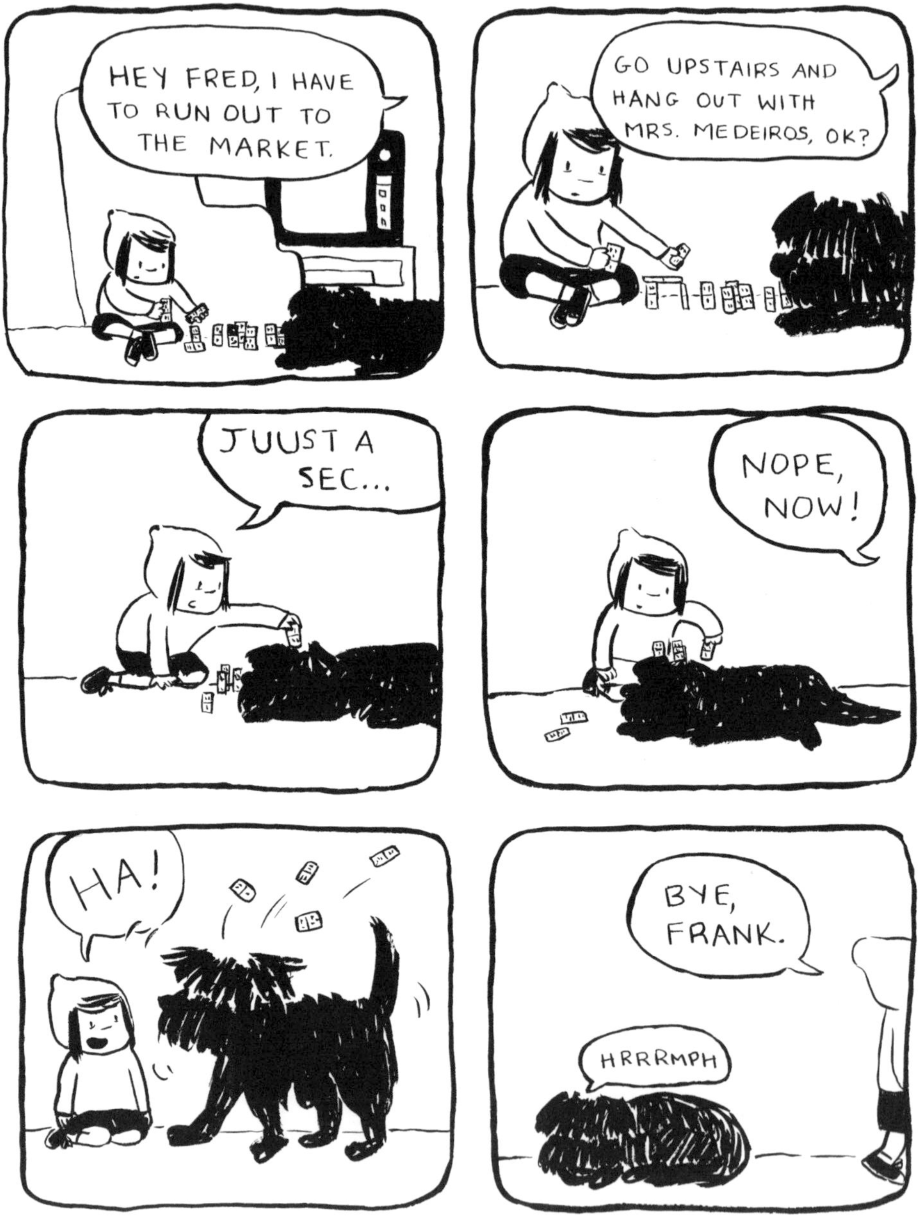
HEY FRED, I HAVE TO RUN OUT TO THE MARKET.
GO UPSTAIRS AND HANG OUT WITH MRS. MEDEIROS, OK?
JUUST A SEC...
NOPE, NOW!
HA!
BYE, FRANK.
HRRRMPH

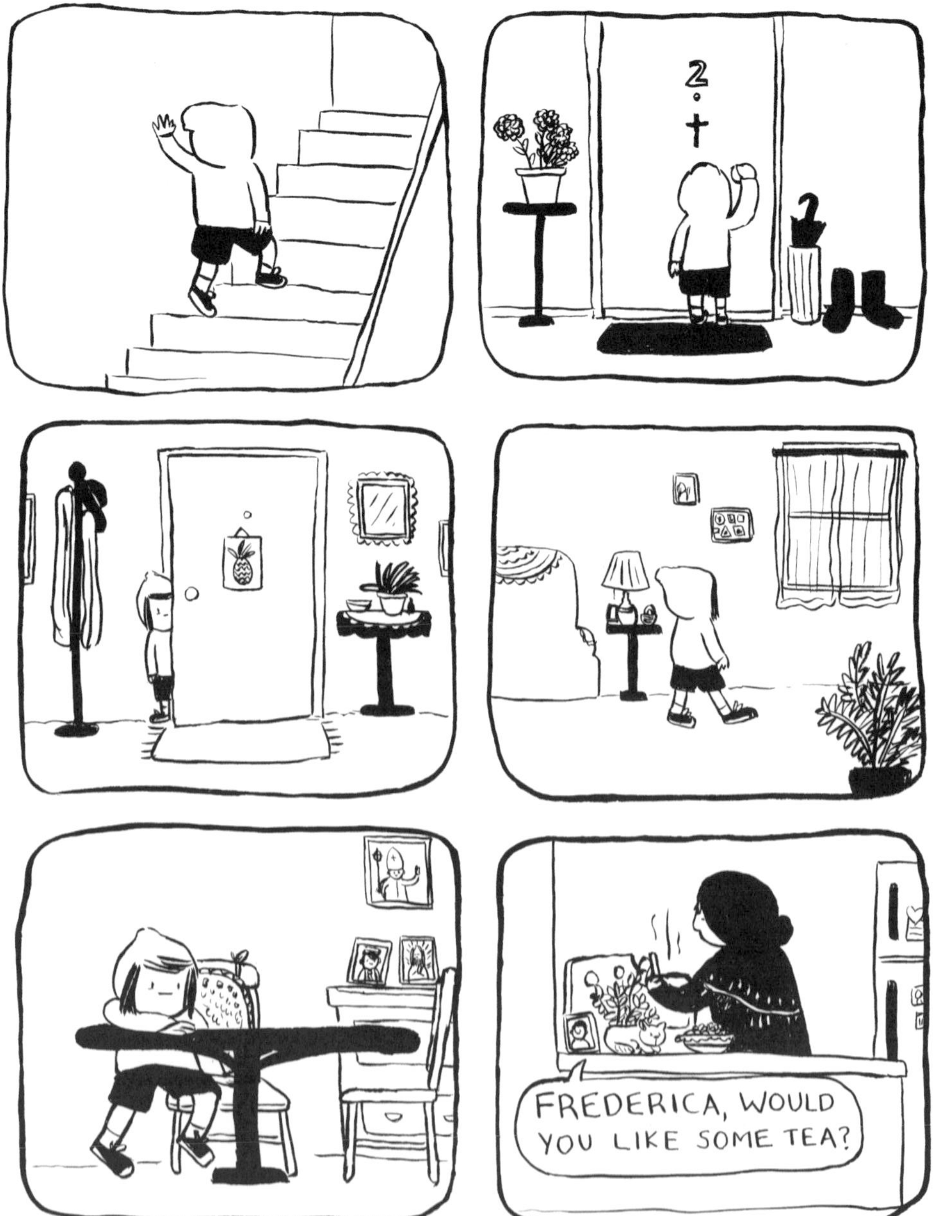
2
FREDERICA, WOULD YOU LIKE SOME TEA?

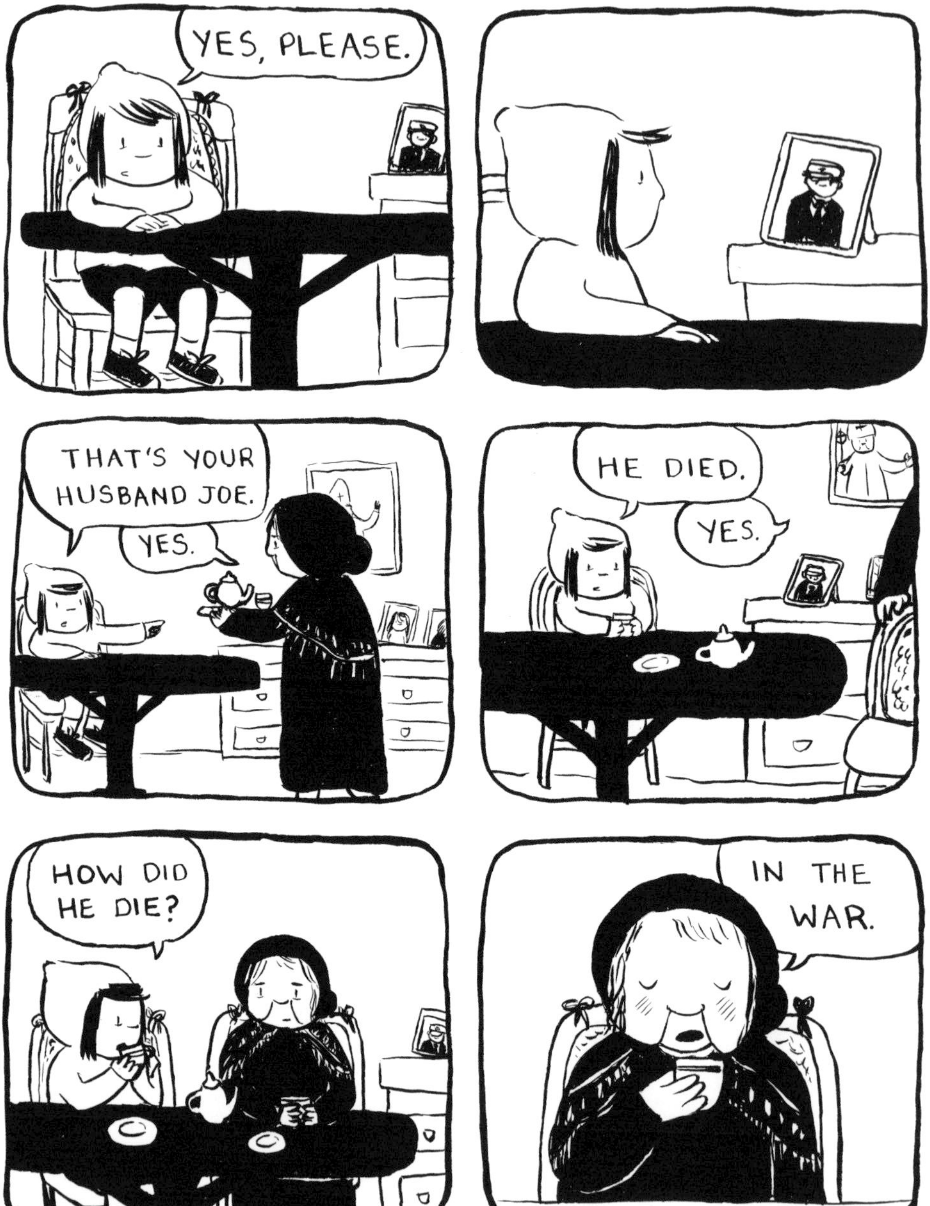
YES, PLEASE.
THAT'S YOUR HUSBAND JOE.
YES.
HE DIED.
YES.
HOW DID HE DIE?
IN THE WAR.

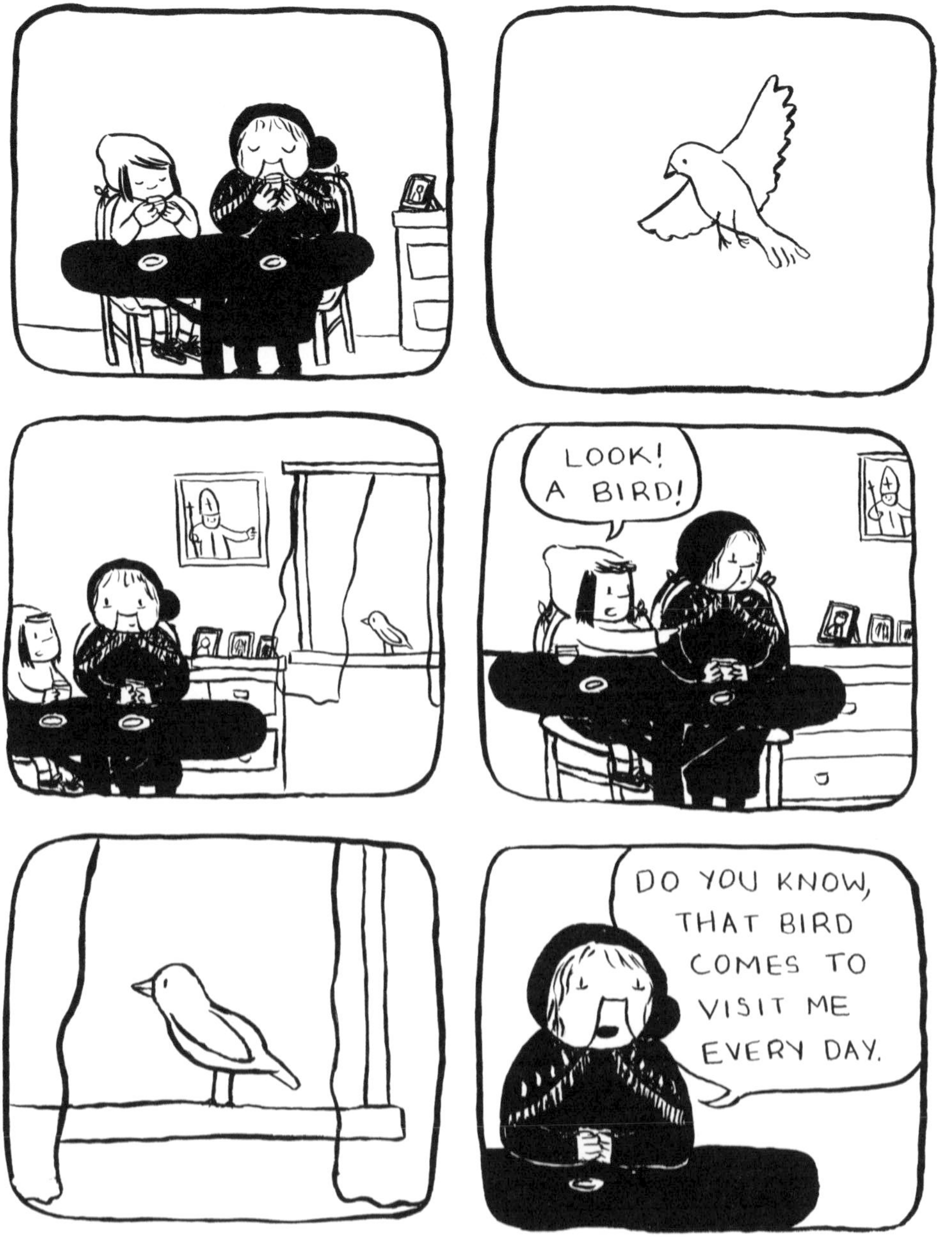
LOOK! A BIRD!
DO YOU KNOW, THAT BIRD COMES TO VISIT ME EVERY DAY.

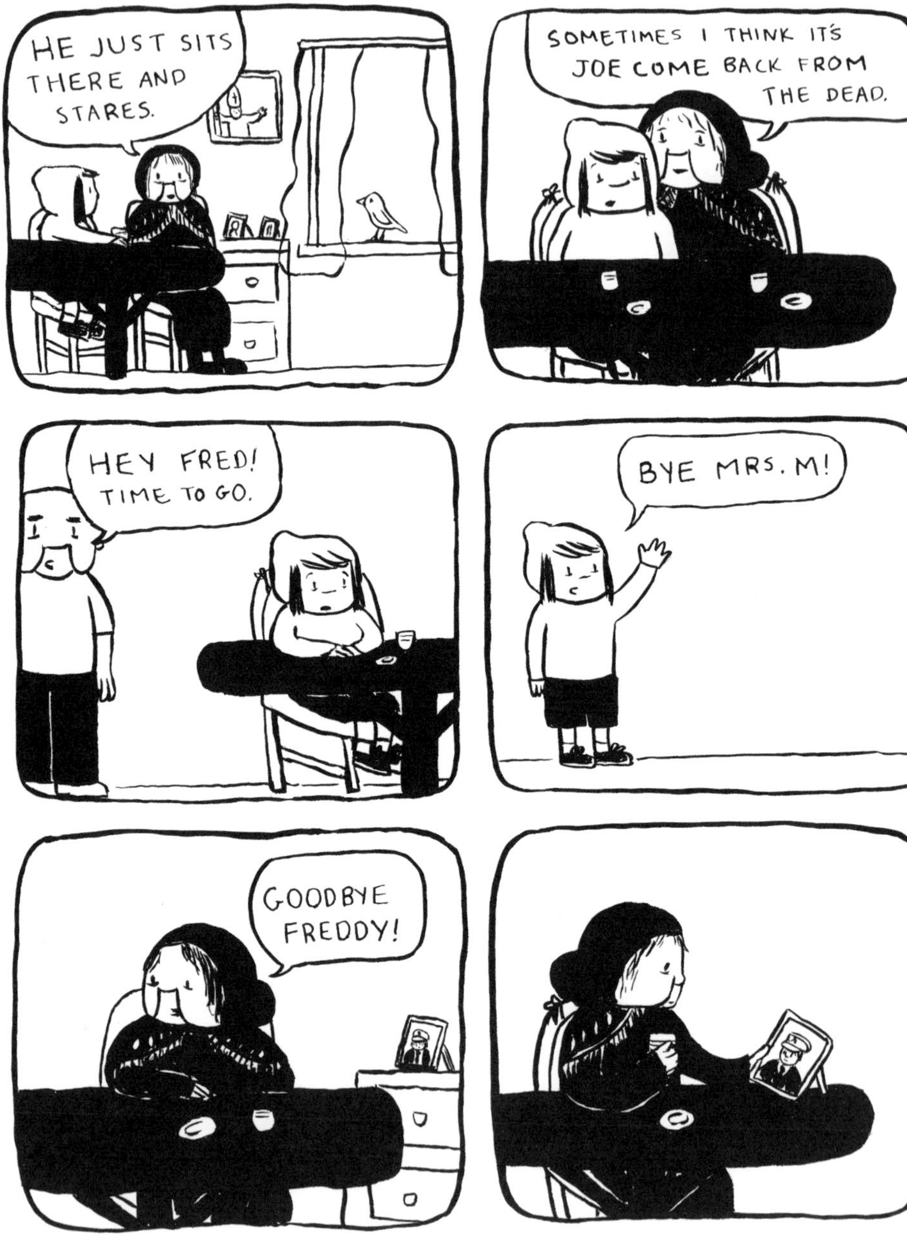
HE JUST SITS THERE AND STARES.
SOMETIMES I THINK IT'S JOE COME BACK FROM THE DEAD.
HEY FRED! TIME TO GO.
BYE MRS. M!
GOODBYE FREDDY!

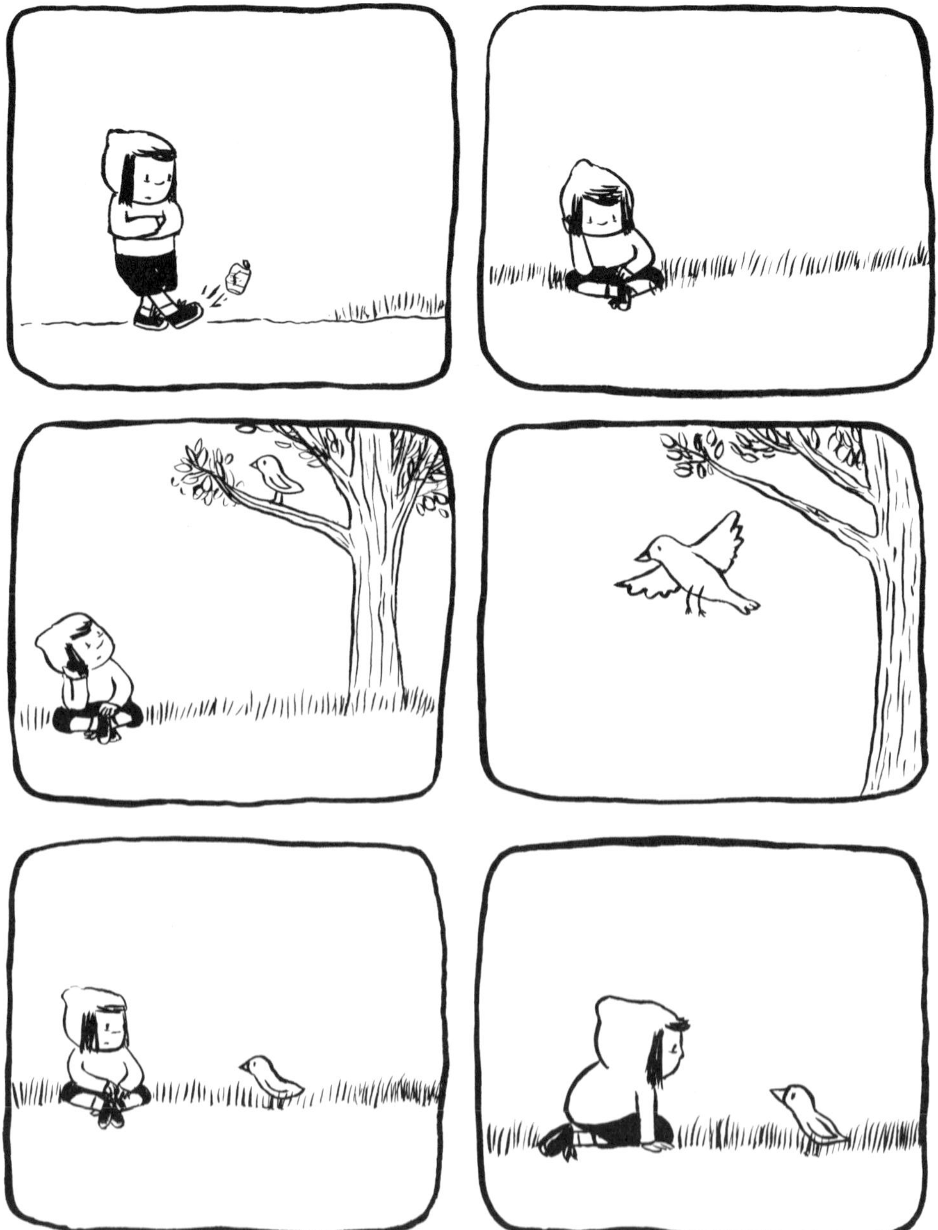

AUNT MARIA

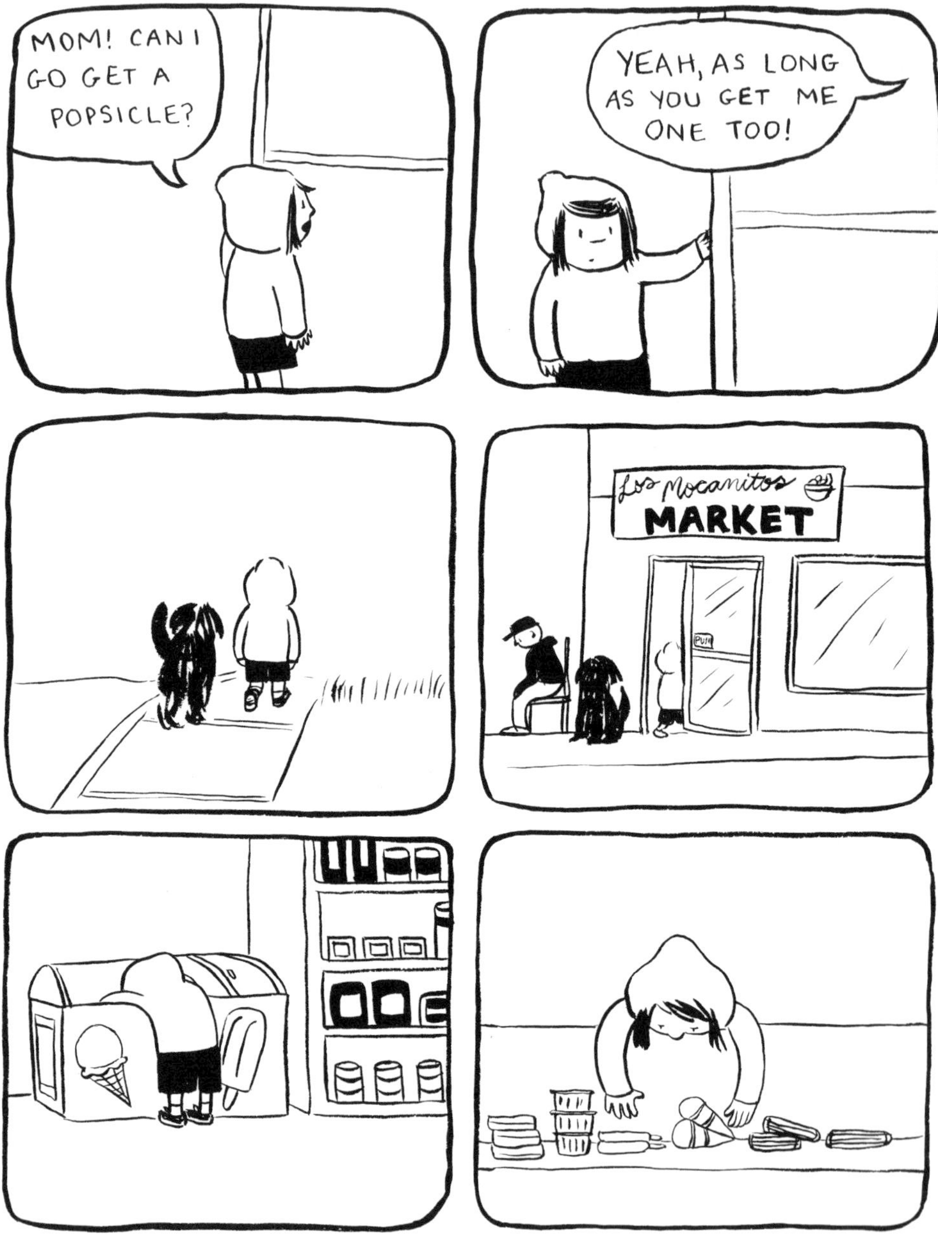
MOM! CAN I GO GET A POPSICLE?
YEAH, AS LONG AS YOU GET ME ONE TOO!
Los Mocanitos
MARKET
PUSH

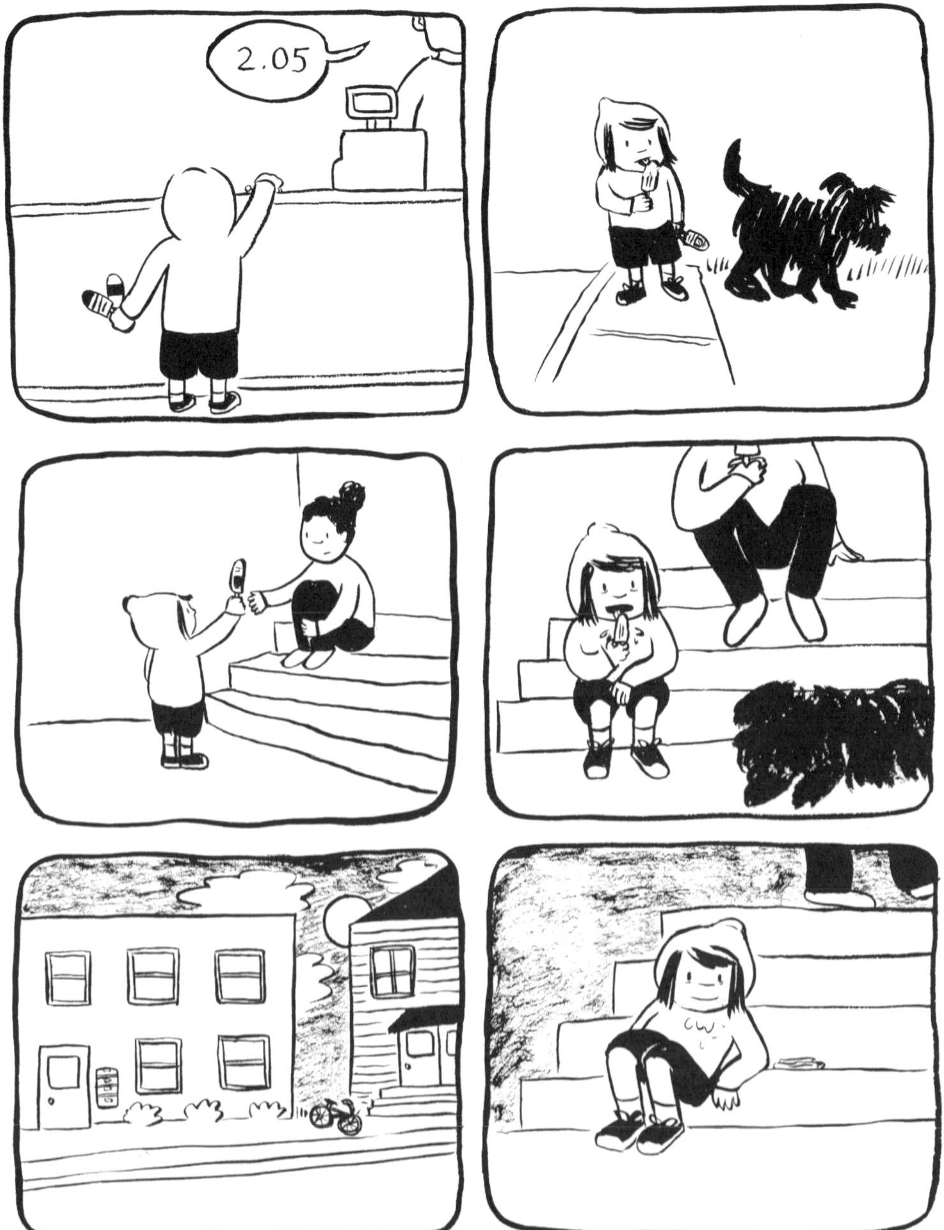
2.05

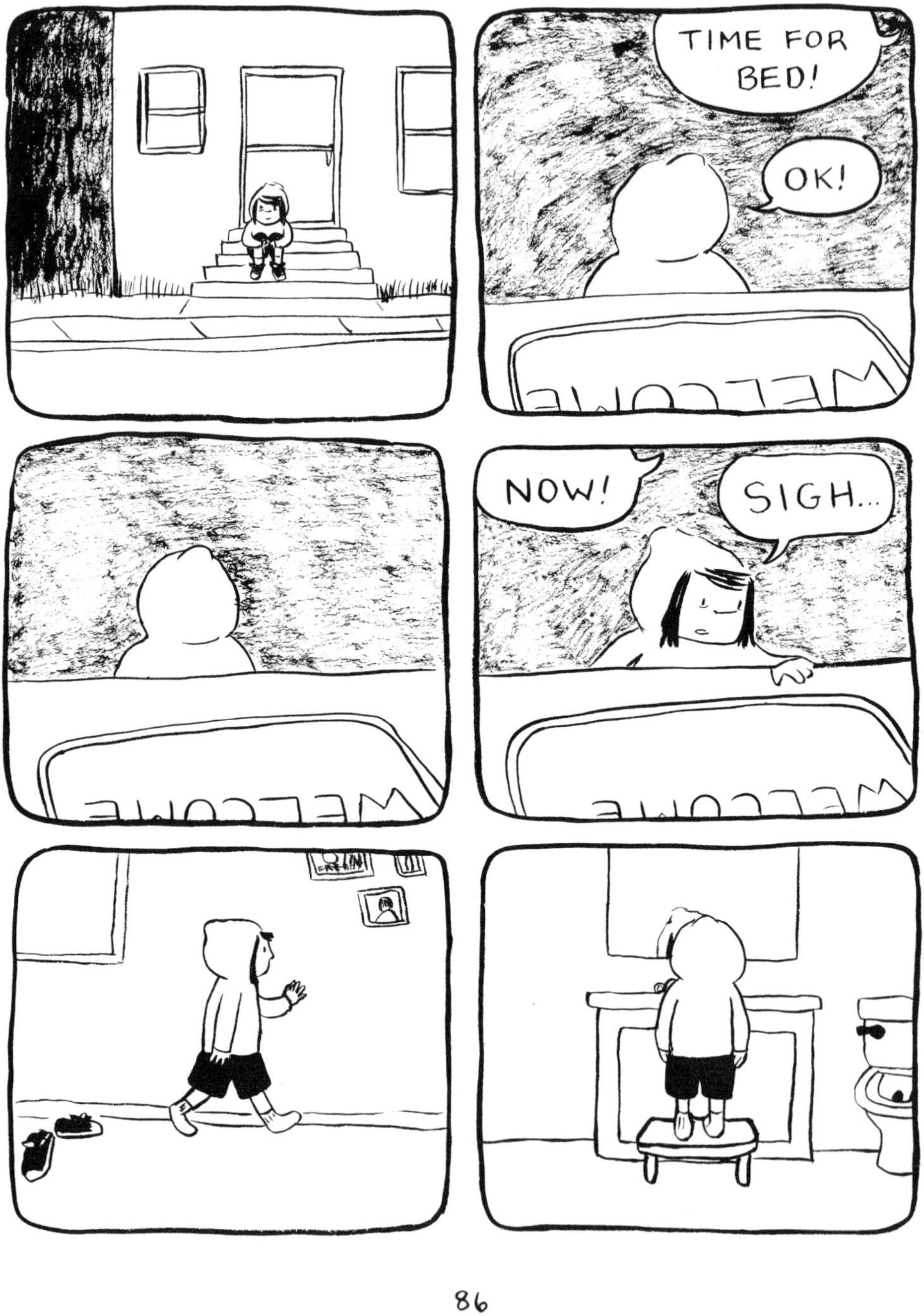
TIME FOR BED!
OK!
NOW!
SIGH...

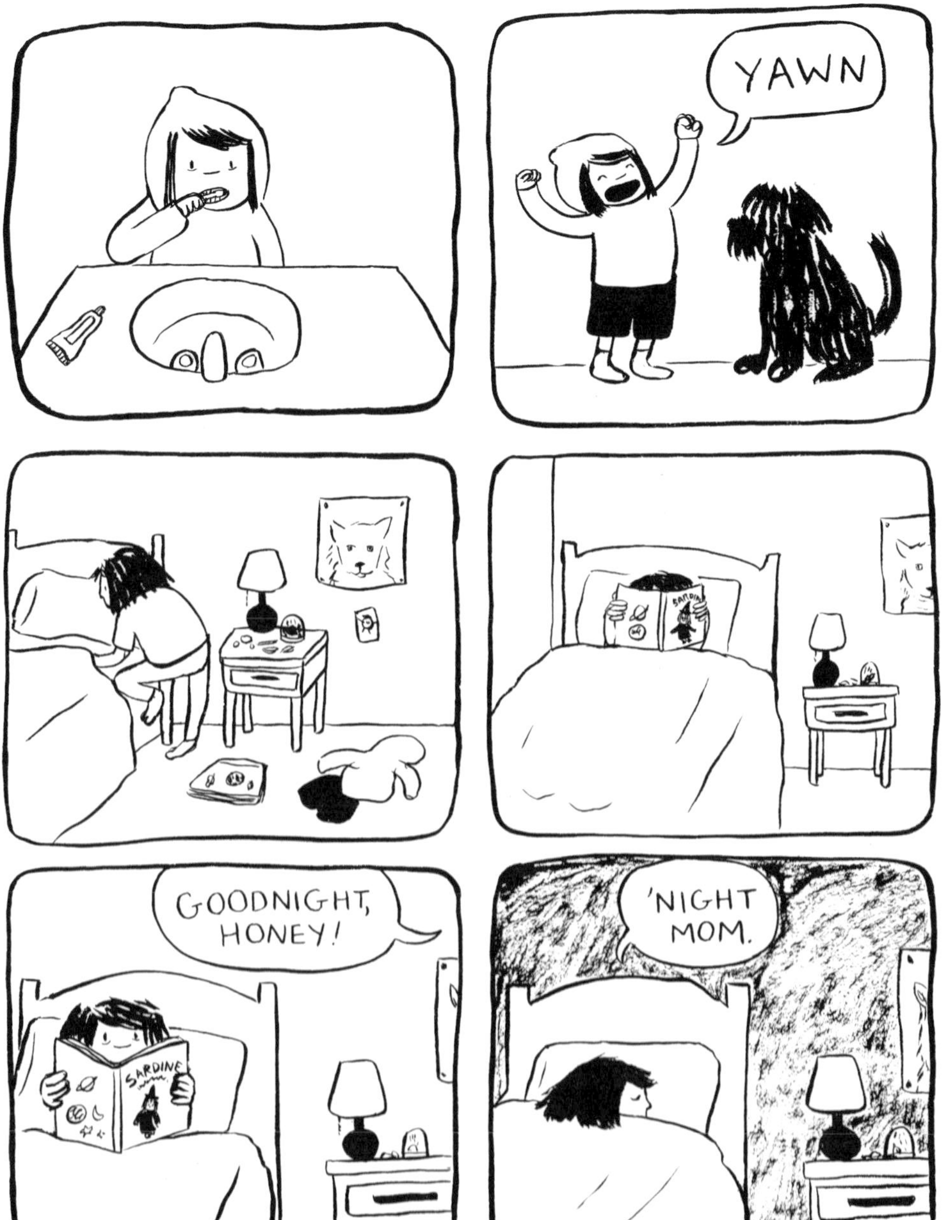
YAWN
SARDINE
SARDINE
GOODNIGHT, HONEY!
'NIGHT MOM.

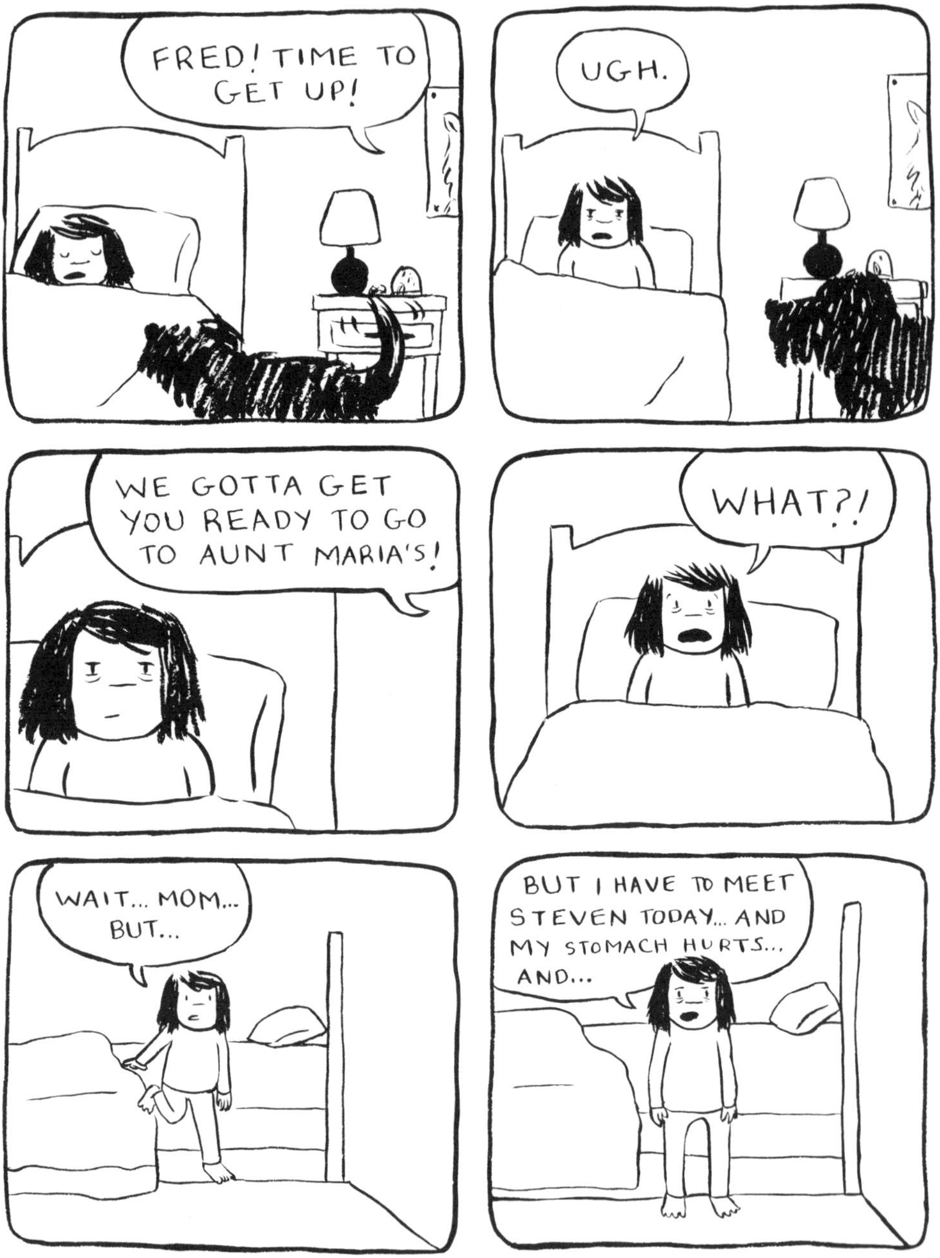

FRED! TIME TO GET UP!
UGH.
WE GOTTA GET YOU READY TO GO TO AUNT MARIA'S!
WHAT?!
WAIT... MOM... BUT...
BUT I HAVE TO MEET STEVEN TODAY... AND MY STOMACH HURTS... AND...

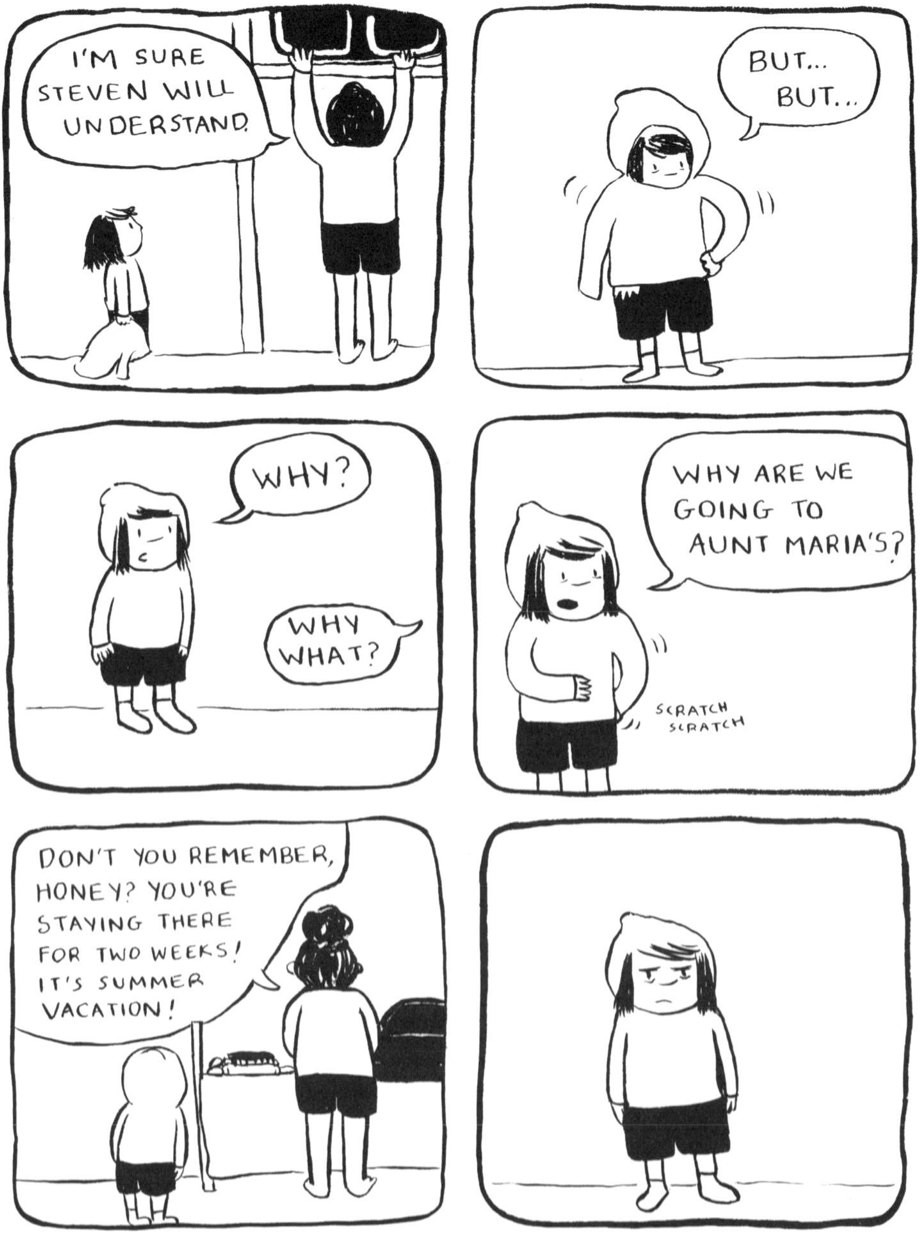
I'M SURE STEVEN WILL UNDERSTAND.
BUT... BUT...
WHY?
WHY WHAT?
WHY ARE WE GOING TO AUNT MARIA'S?
SCRATCH SCRATCH
DON'T YOU REMEMBER, HONEY? YOU'RE STAYING THERE FOR TWO WEEKS! IT'S SUMMER VACATION!

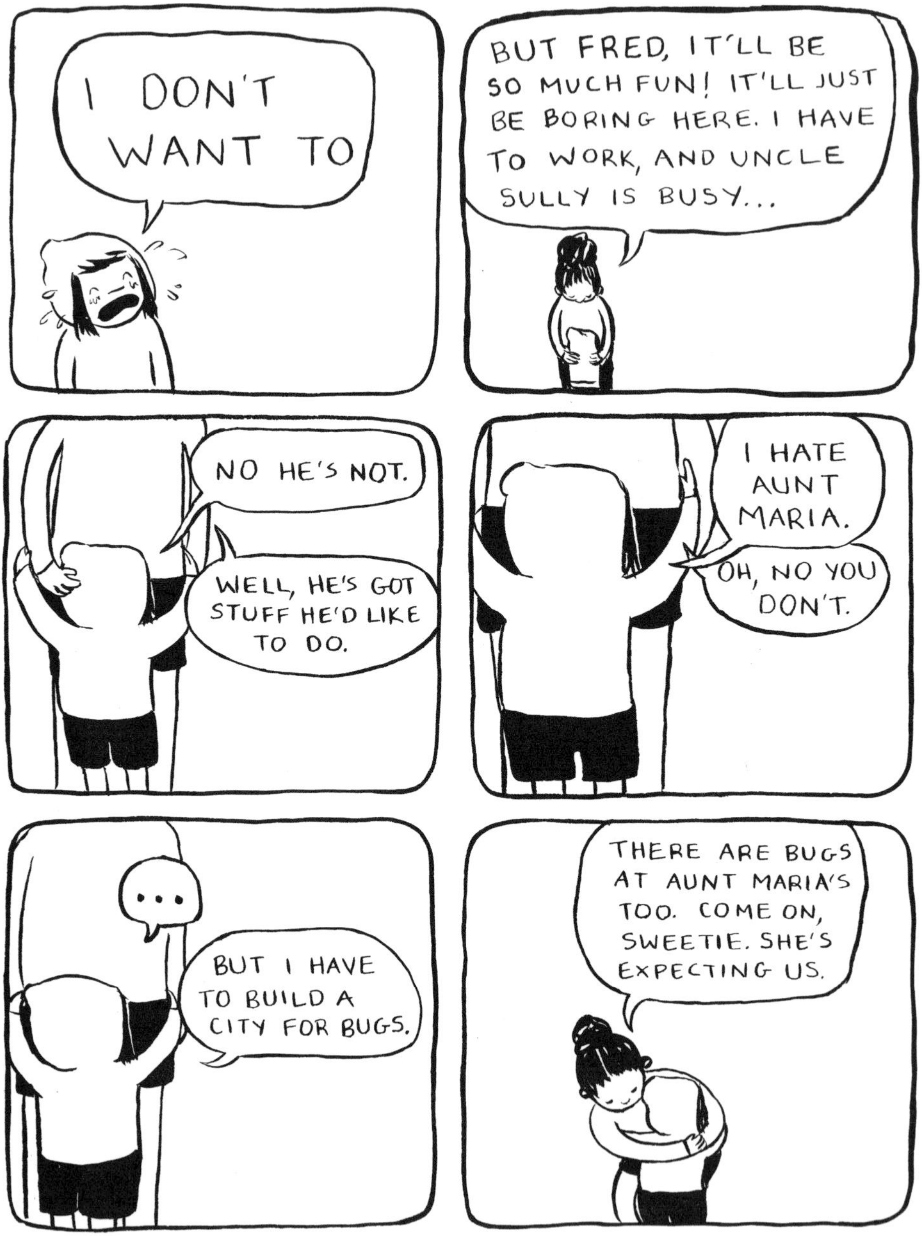
I DON'T WANT TO
BUT FRED, IT'LL BE SO MUCH FUN! IT'LL JUST BE BORING HERE. I HAVE TO WORK, AND UNCLE SULLY IS BUSY...
NO HE'S NOT.
WELL, HE'S GOT STUFF HE'D LIKE TO DO.
I HATE AUNT MARIA.
OH, NO YOU DON'T.
...
BUT I HAVE TO BUILD A CITY FOR BUGS.
THERE ARE BUGS AT AUNT MARIA'S TOO. COME ON, SWEETIE. SHE'S EXPECTING US.

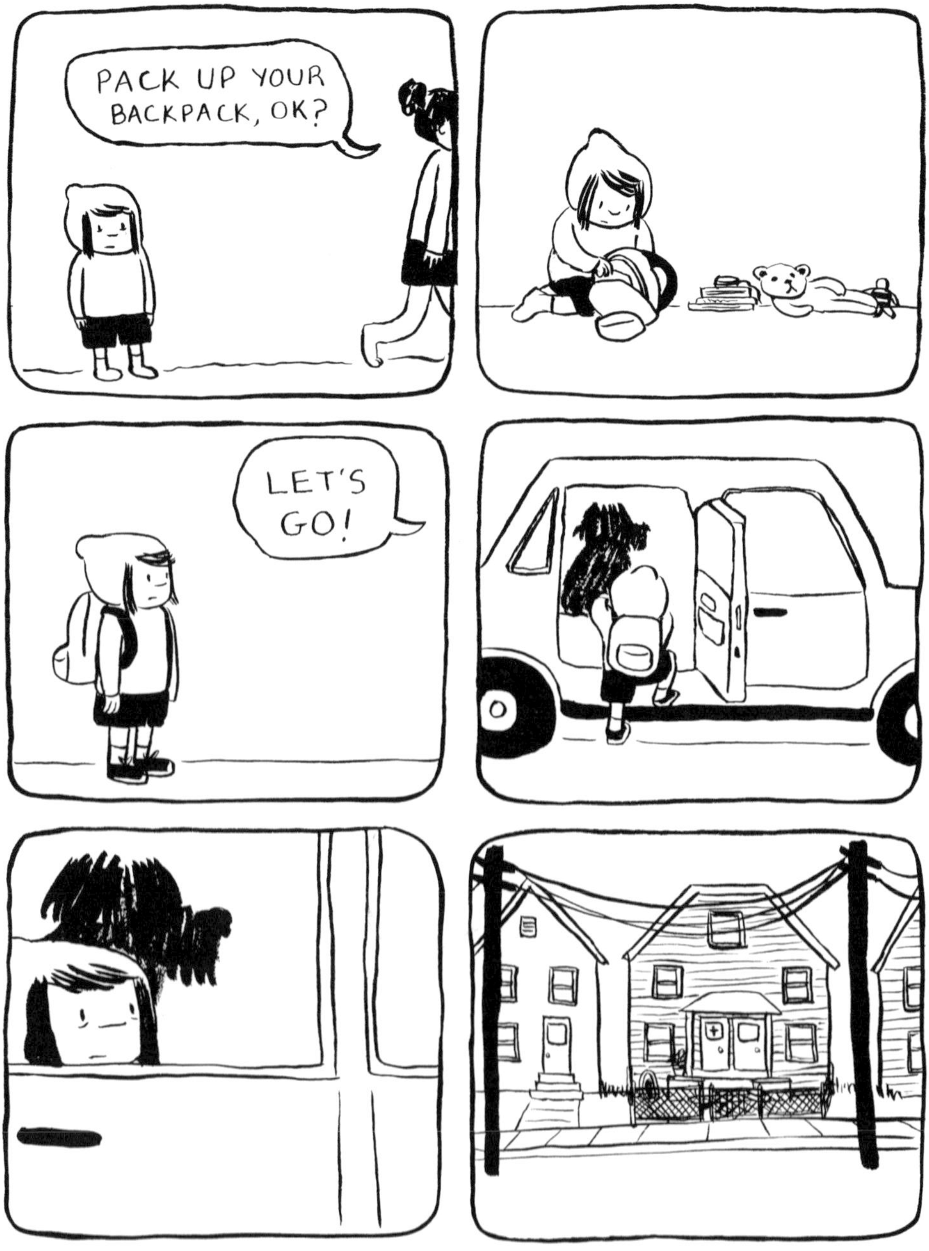
PACK UP YOUR BACKPACK, OK?
LET'S GO!

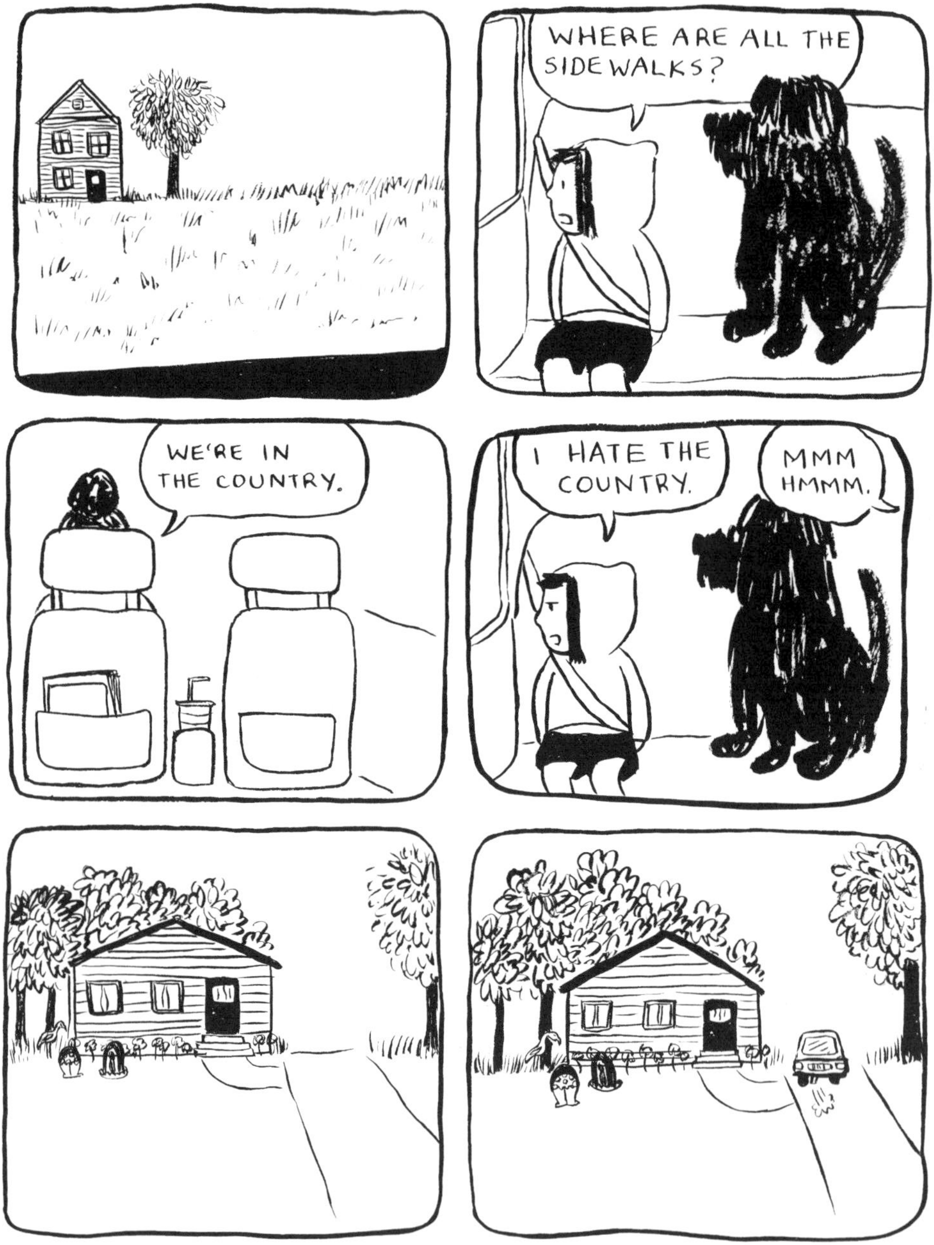
WHERE ARE ALL THE SIDEWALKS?
WE'RE IN THE COUNTRY.
I HATE THE COUNTRY.
MMM HMMM.

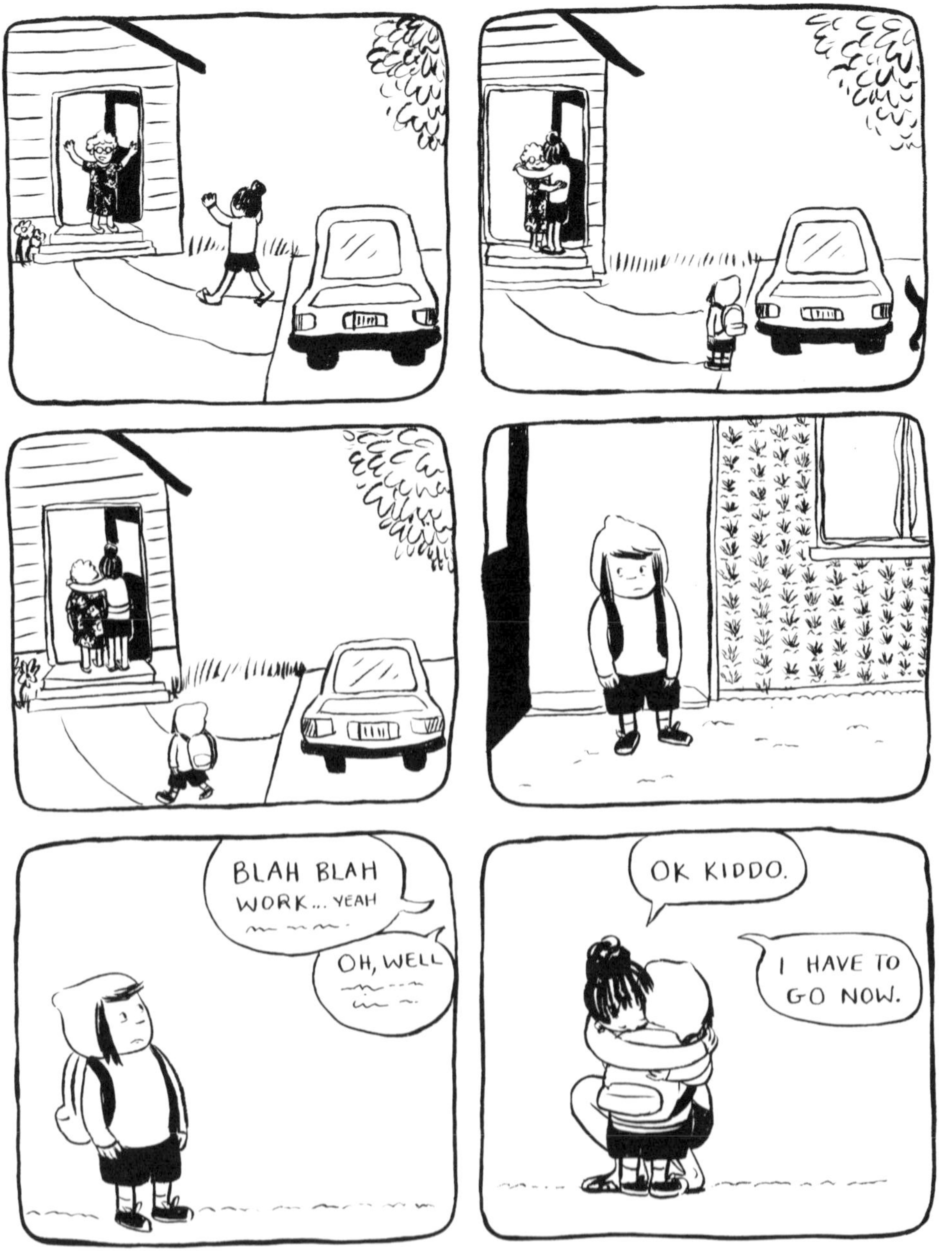
BLAH BLAH WORK... YEAH
OH, WELL
OK KIDDO.
I HAVE TO GO NOW.

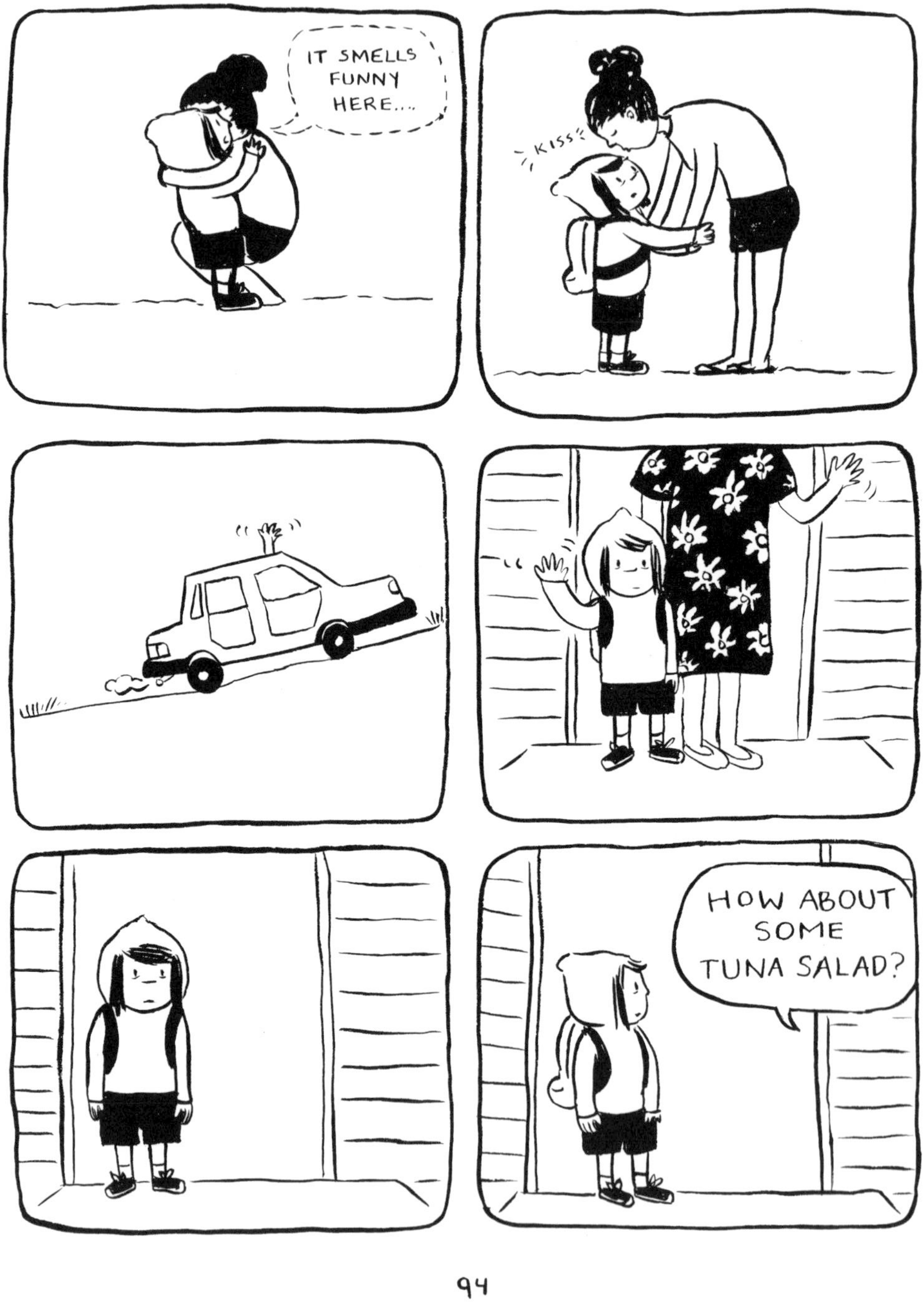
IT SMELLS FUNNY HERE....
KISS
HOW ABOUT SOME TUNA SALAD?

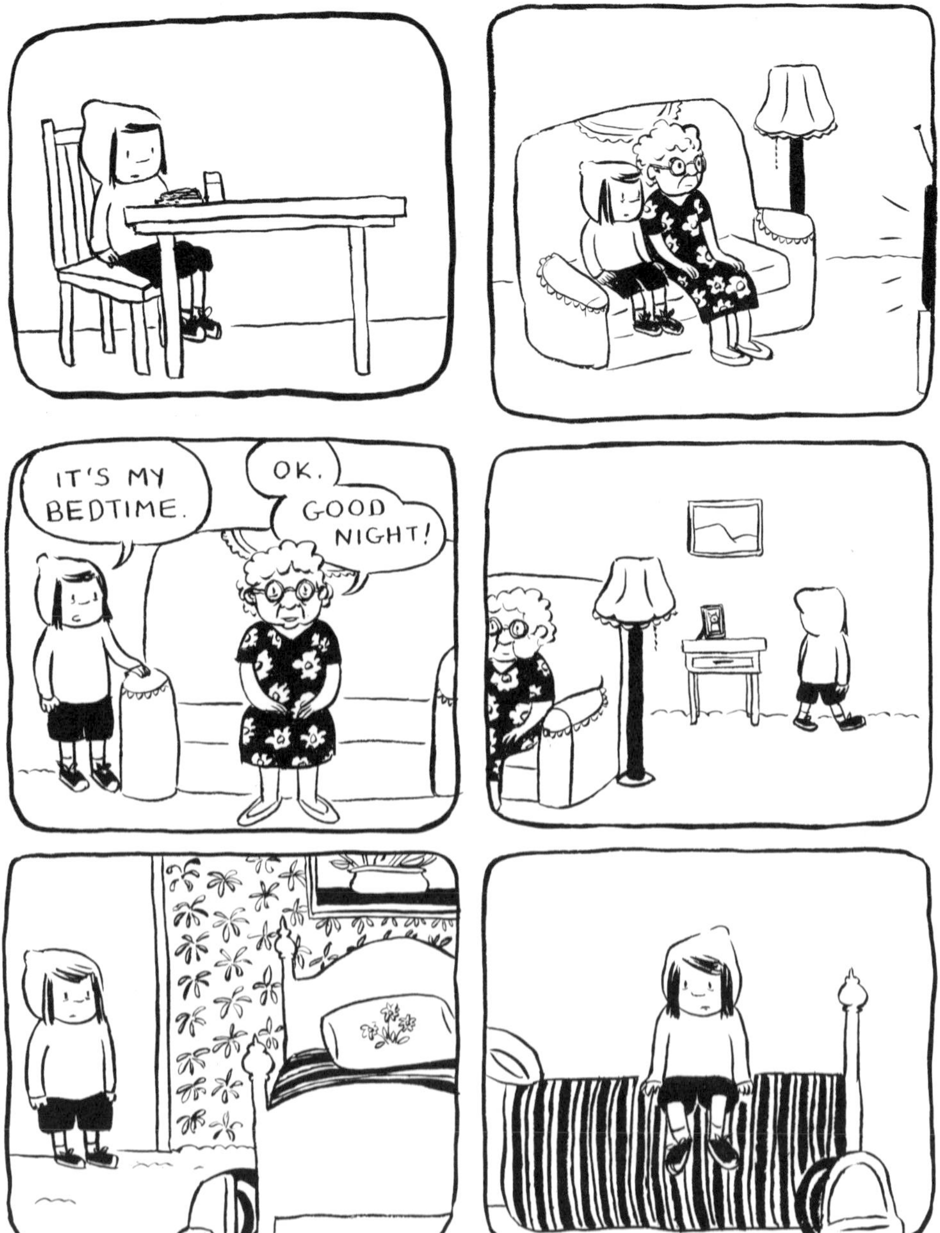
IT'S MY BEDTIME.
OK.
GOOD NIGHT!

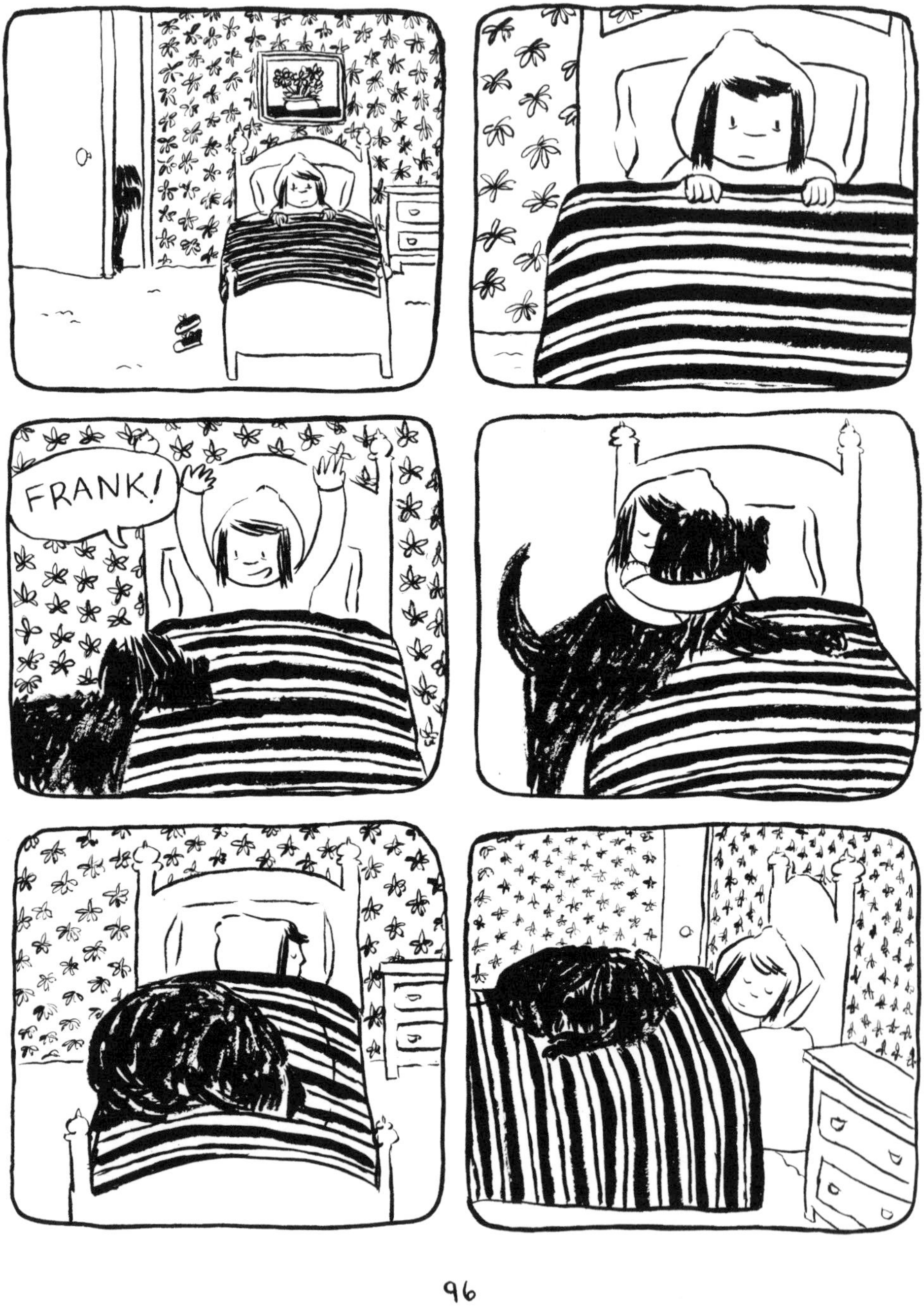
FRANK!

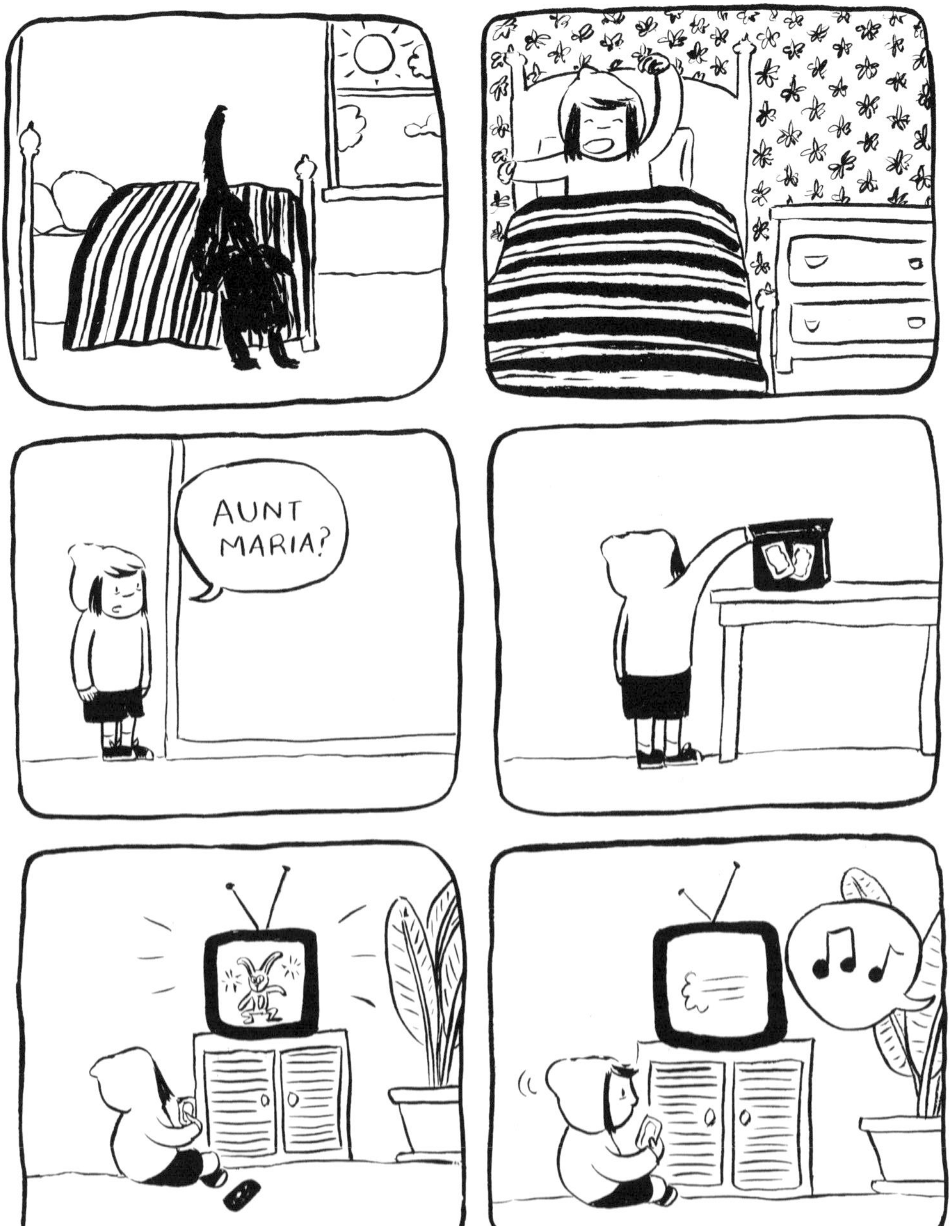
AUNT MARIA?

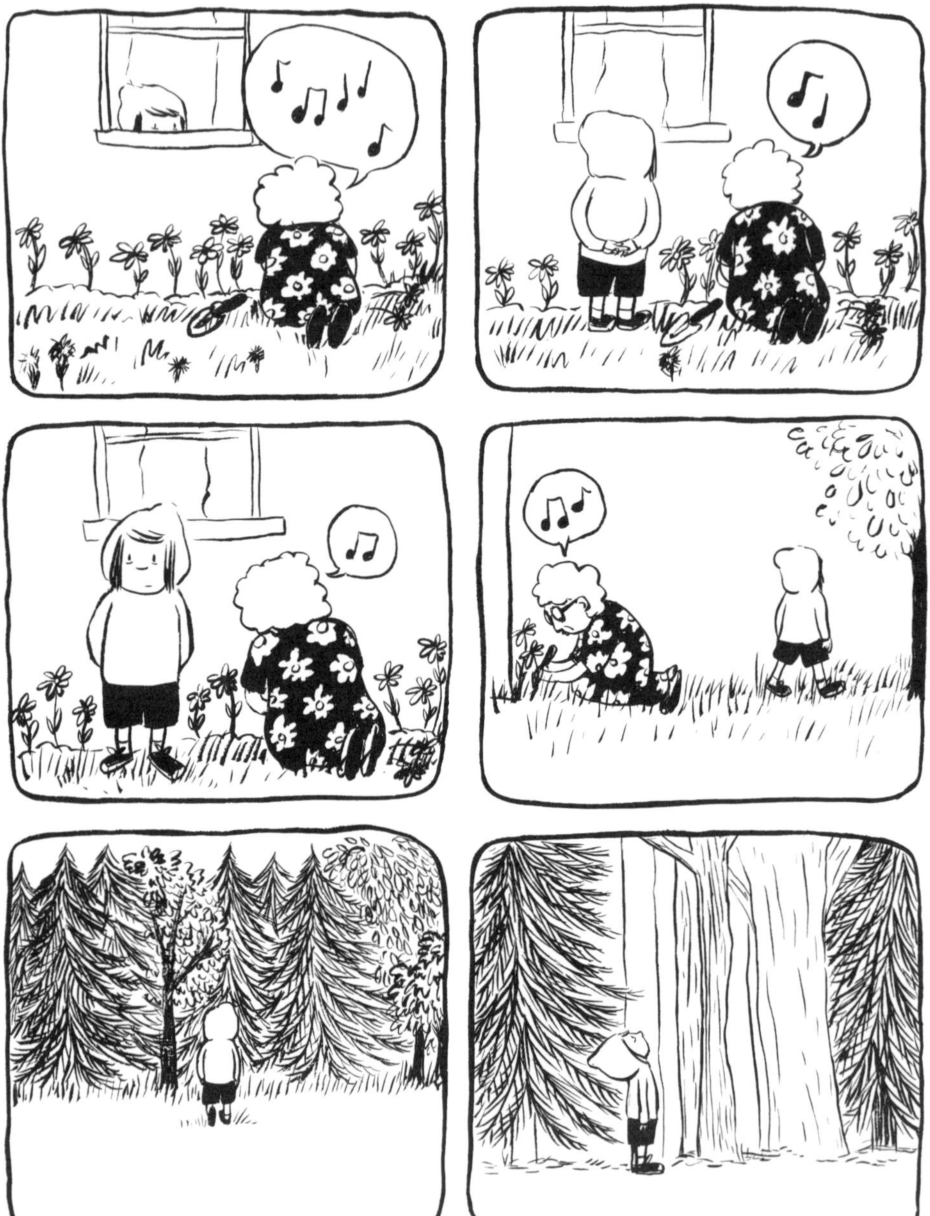

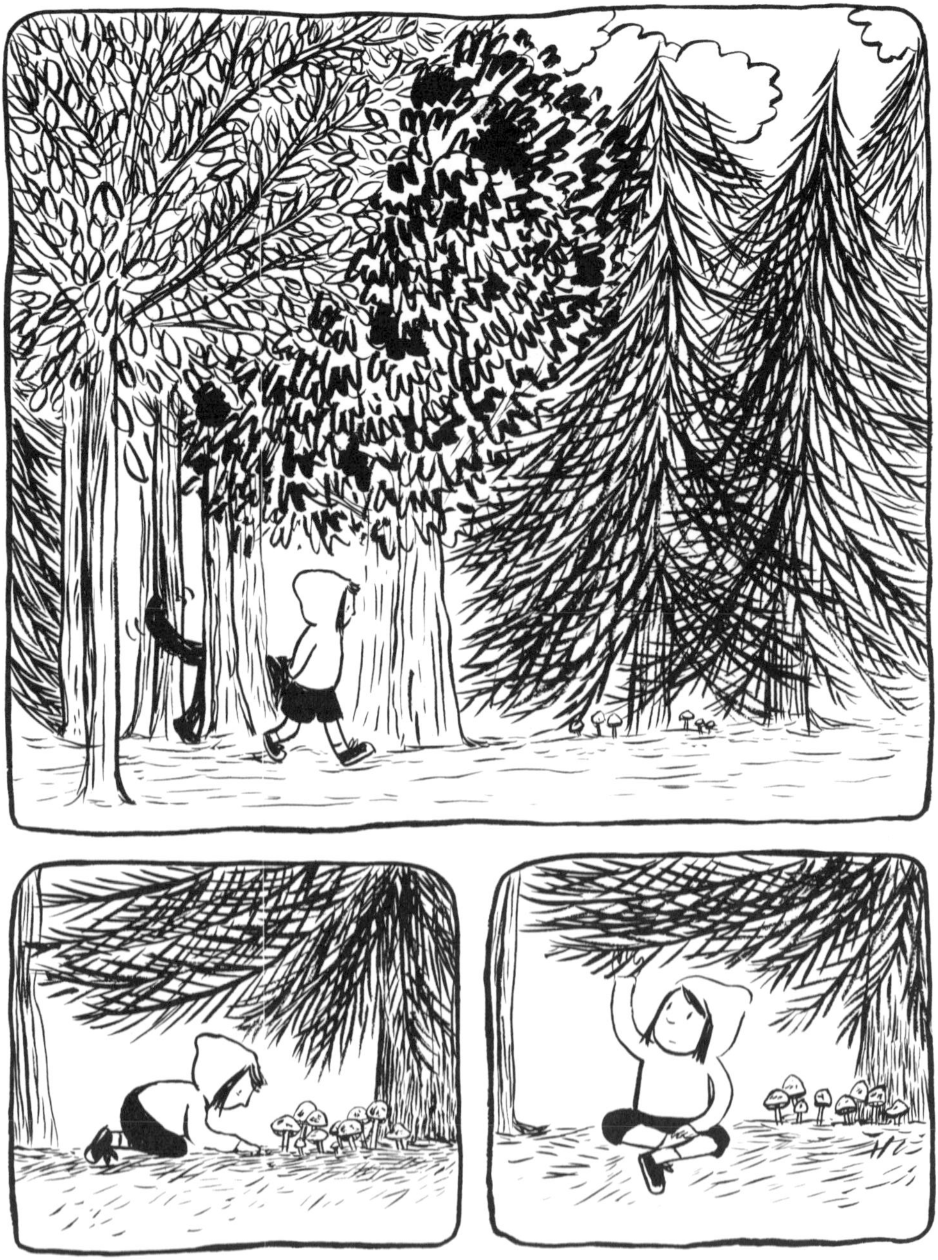

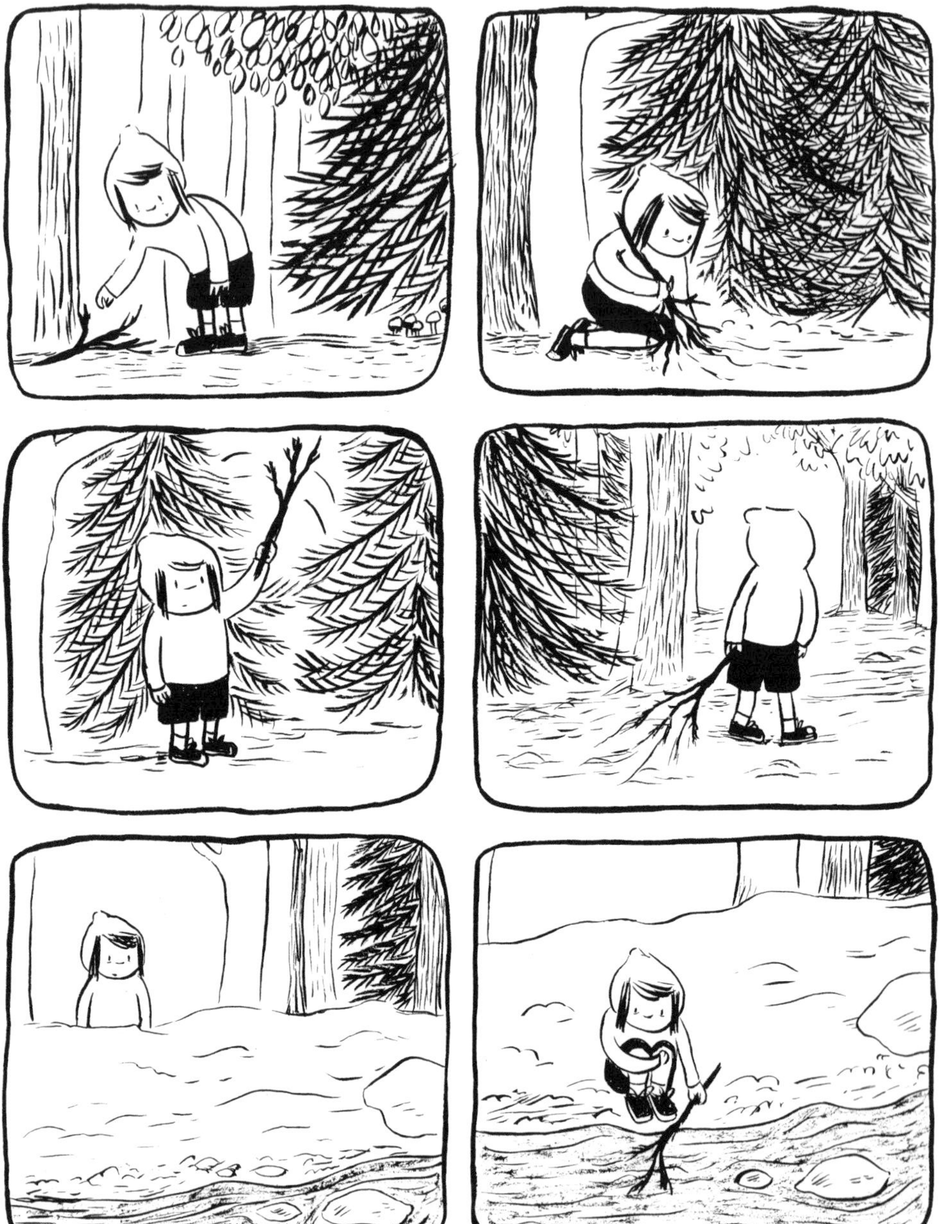

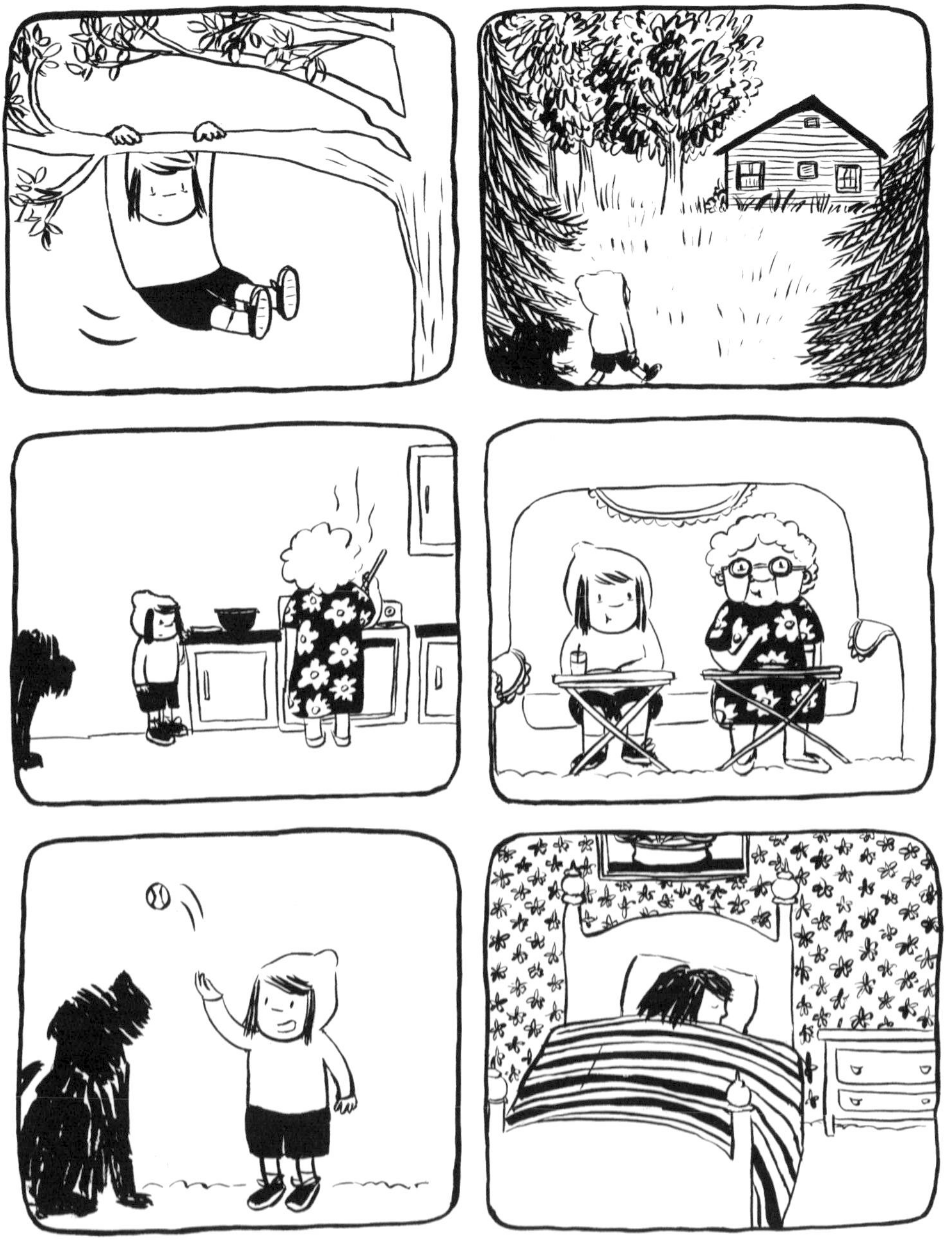

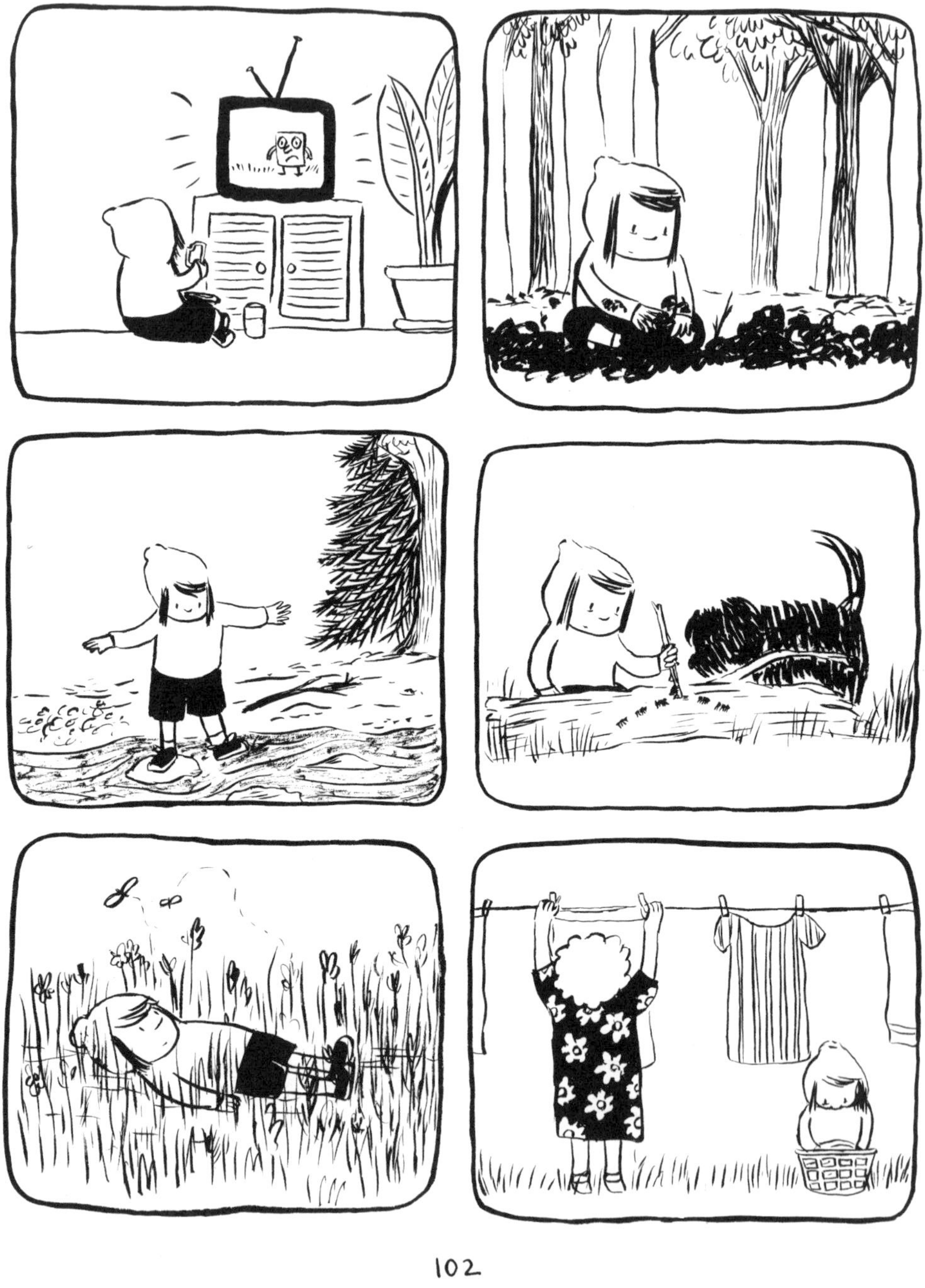

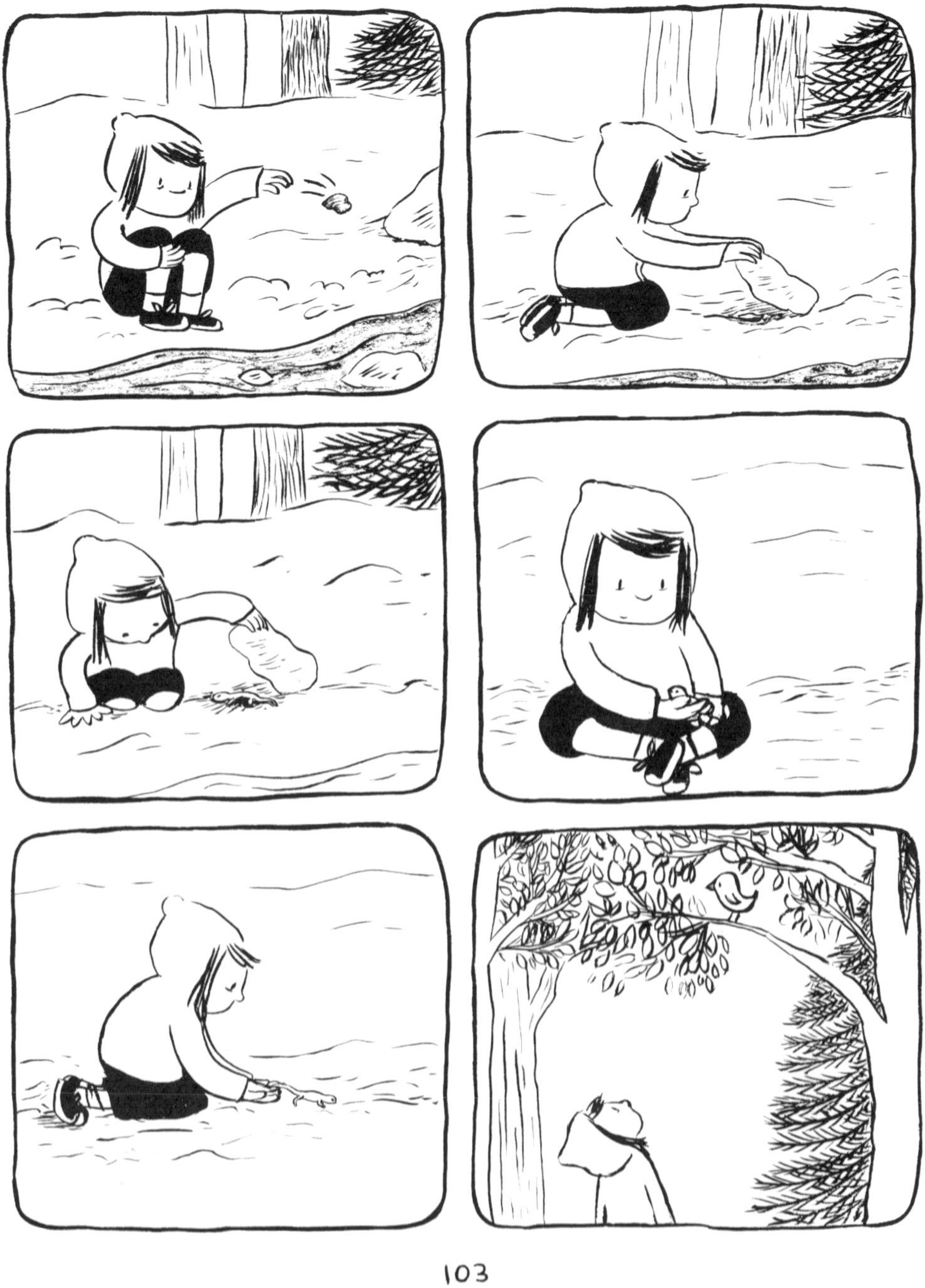

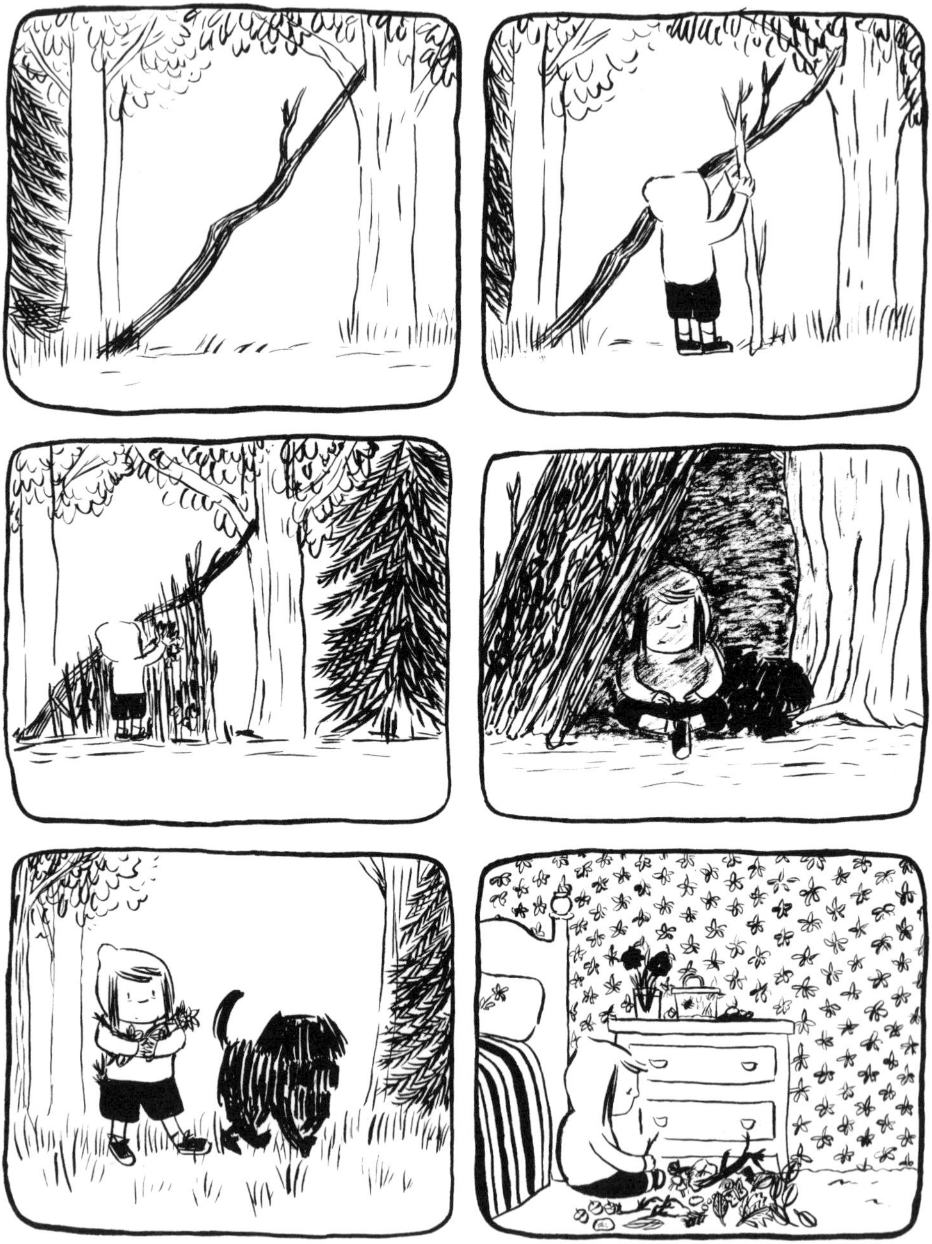

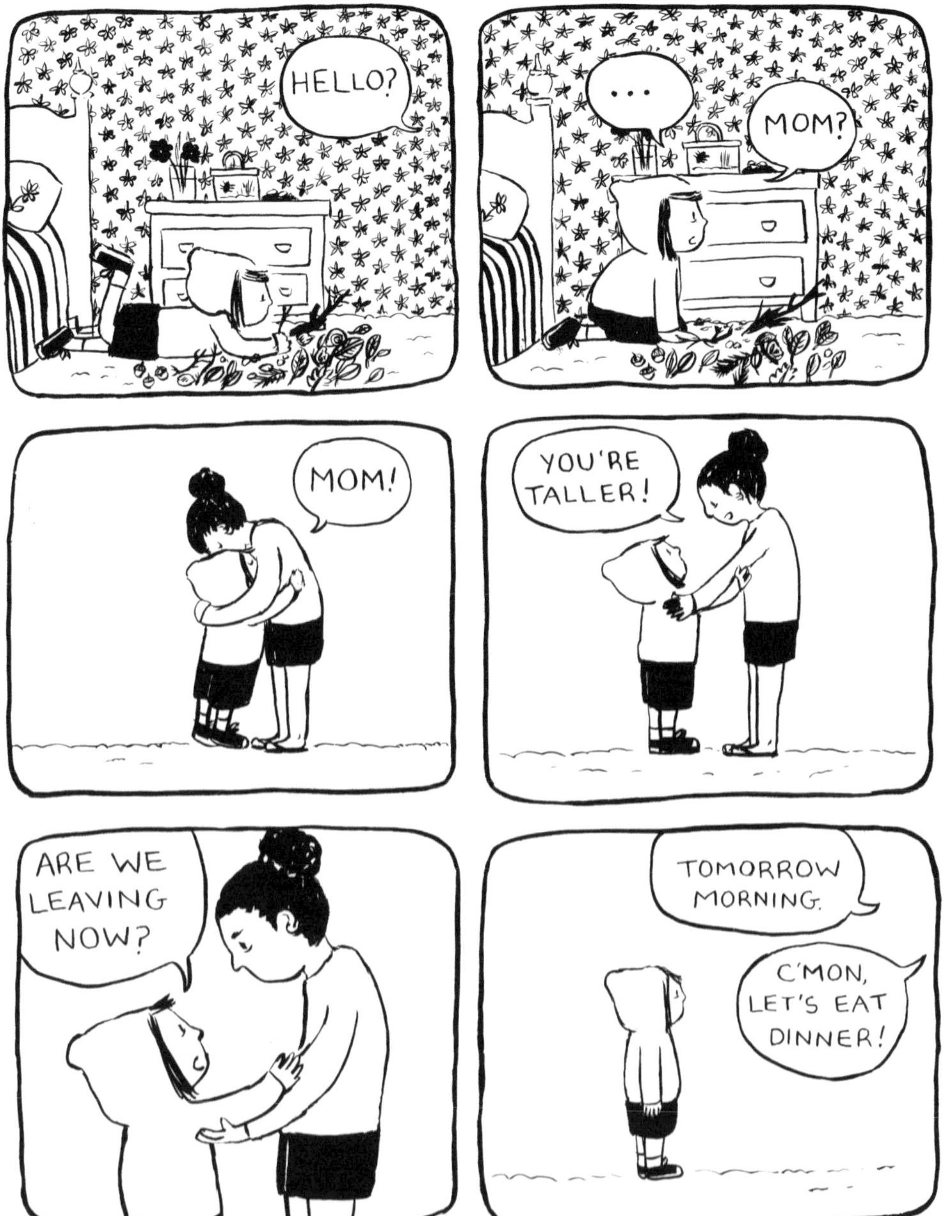
HELLO?
...
MOM?
MOM!
YOU'RE TALLER!
ARE WE LEAVING NOW?
TOMORROW MORNING.
C'MON, LET'S EAT DINNER!

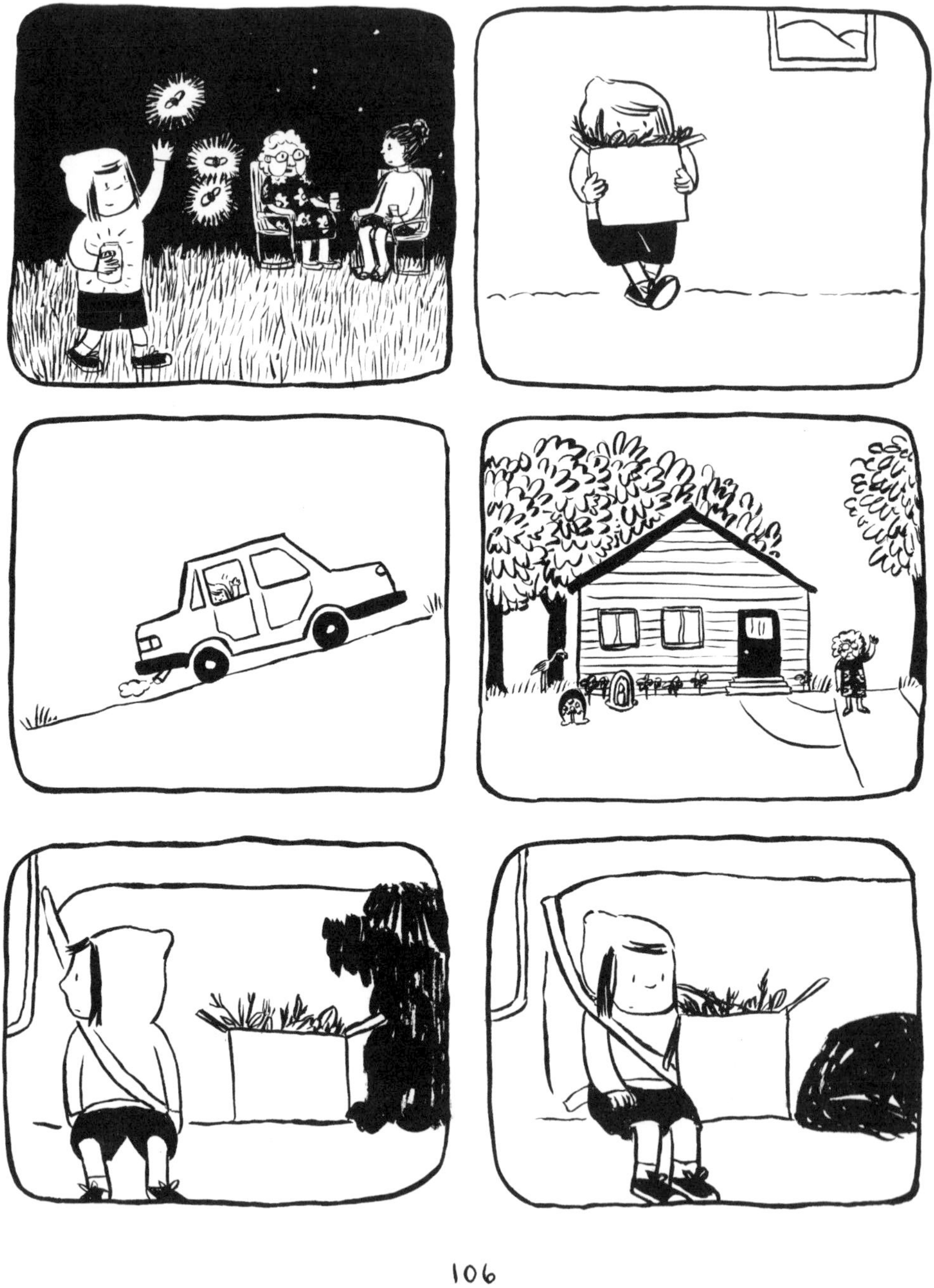

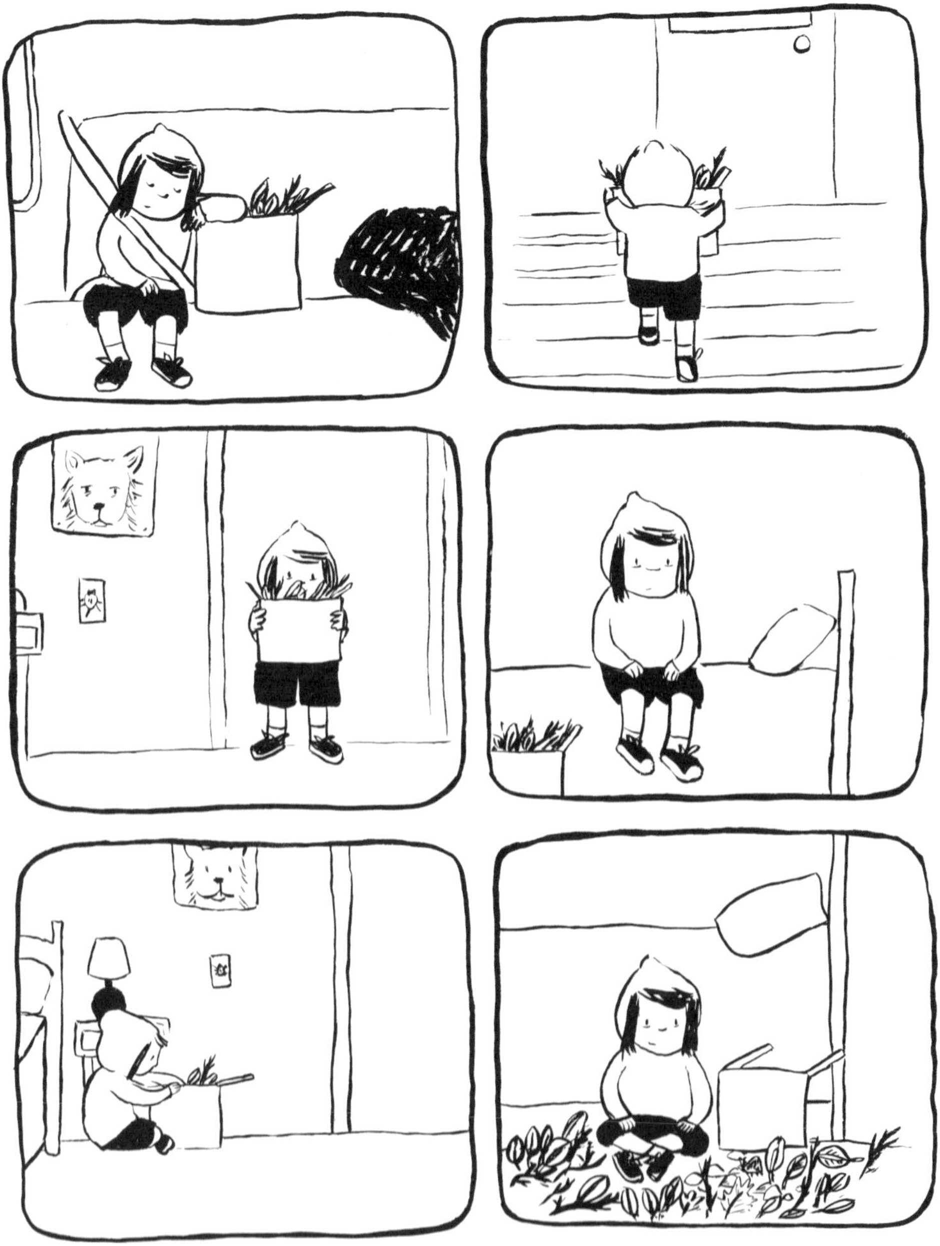

A million thanks to Chuck, my family, my friends, CCS, James Sturm and family, the Xeric Foundation, and you. ♡

Melissa Mendes grew up in the
woods of western Massachusetts.
She graduated from The Center
for Cartoon Studies in 2010.
She has done a bunch of
mini-comics, but this is her
first book.

mendes.me @ gmail.com
www.mmmendes.com

Freddy Stories © 2011
by Melissa Mendes

www.mmmendes.com
mendes.me@gmail.com

ISBN: 978-0-9835942-1-5

First printing: August 2011

Printed in Canada

Published through a
generous grant from
the Xeric Foundation!
www.xericfoundation.org

For wholesale contact:
shenton4sales@aol.com